Controversies in Sociology

edited by
Professor T. B. Bottomore and Dr M. J. Mulkay

7

Marx and the End of
Orientalism

Controversies in Sociology

Marx and the End of Orientalism

BRYAN S. TURNER

Senior Lecturer in Sociology, University of Aberdeen

London
GEORGE ALLEN & UNWIN
Boston   Sydney

First published in 1978

GEORGE ALLEN & UNWIN LTD
40 Museum Street, London WC1A 1LU

© George Allen & Unwin (Publishers) Ltd, 1978

British Library Cataloguing in Publication Data

Turner, Bryan Stanley
    Marx and the end of Orientalism. — (Controversies in sociology; 7).
    1. Communism and Islam   2. Islamic countries — Social conditions
    I. Title   II. Series
    309.1'17'671   HX550.18   78-40476

    ISBN 0-04-321020-1
    ISBN 0-04-321021-X Pbk

Typeset in 10 on 11 point Times by Red Lion Setters
and printed in Great Britain
by Unwin Brothers Limited
The Gresham Press, Old Woking, Surrey

In memory of my father

Contents

Acknowledgements

It would have been impossible to complete this study without the active support of the 'Hull group' for Middle East studies (especially Talal Asad, Roger Owen, David Seddon and David Waines) which is the main organ in Britain for the critique of Orientalism. I have derived enormous benefit from sharp disagreements with Sami Zubaida over what does or does not constitute a problem for Marxism. For their patient attempts to correct my ideological views of social reality, I am grateful to Nicholas Abercrombie, John Martin, Susan Shipley and John Urry at the University of Lancaster. Tom Bottomore and Mike Mulkay have been generous in providing encouragement and guidance over the contents and organisation of this book. My principal thanks, however, go to my wife without whose domestic labour all of this would have been in vain.

Aberdeen, 1978

Introduction

The study of the Middle East lags behind other area studies in both theoretical and substantive terms. The debates in social science over the characteristics of underdevelopment and dependency were largely stimulated by problems in the analysis of Latin America. Similarly, such socioeconomic theories as the dual economy and the plural society were initially developed as perspectives for the study of Asian social structures. There have been few seminal theoretical debates in connection with the sociological analysis of Middle East societies. Indeed, it is doubtful whether the study of the Middle East has contributed in any significant way to the analytical development of those disciplines which constitute Middle East area studies; although it may be that anthropology, in terms of the analysis of feuding, honour and nomadic pastoralism, is exempt from this negative judgement (Antoun, 1976). In this study of Marxist perspectives on the Middle East, the general relevance of the Asiatic mode of production (hereafter, AMP) will play a part in subsequent discussion. However, the AMP was not a theoretical model generated by Marx and Engels solely for the analysis of the Middle East (Melotti, 1977). In his article on 'The British Rule in India' (Marx and Engels, 1972), Marx refers to the importance of geographical conditions 'extending from the Sahara, through Arabia, Persia, India and Tartary' in his initial formulation of the AMP. The primary focus of subsequent debates about the AMP has been India, China and Russia (Sofri, 1969). Within sociology, Max Weber's theory of patrimonialism, which has close analytical similarities with the Marxist concept of the AMP, was formulated with special reference to Ottoman Turkey. The principal developments of the concepts of patrimonial domination and 'Sultanism' have, however, been stimulated by and in reference to Asia (Tambiah, 1976) rather than by Middle East area studies.

These observations do not mean, of course, that there is no tradition of social science analysis of the Middle East and North Africa, but merely that Middle East area studies are underdeveloped and, as we shall see, riddled by ideological and conceptual difficulties. An additional difficulty is that there is an underdeveloped indigenous tradition of sociological analysis. While legitimate claims can be made about the significance of Ibn Khaldun as a social theorist (Turner, 1971; al-Qazzaz, 1972), *The Muqaddimah* has not been employed as an effective framework for sociological inquiry. The Middle East does, however, possess an imported, European tradition which was initially created as an intellectual aid to colonial rule, especially in the Maghreb. The anthropological analysis of tribal groupings, political structure, religious fraternities and the *makhzan-siba* dichotomy (Gellner and Micaud, 1973) was largely a response to the administrative needs of French colonialism. As a result of this colonial intervention, the dominant mode of sociological analysis amongst indigenous, professional sociologists is Durkheimian. This influence of Durkheimian sociology is considerable amongst French-trained sociologists in Algeria and Tunisia, but it has also had a profound impact on sociology and historical scholarship in Turkey through the pioneering work of Ziya Gökalp (Ülken, 1950) and Fuat Köprülü. Apart from the general issue of the theoretical adequacy of Durkheimian sociology as such, the dependence of indigenous sociology on an external, post-colonial intellectual tradition creates sensitive academic and professional problems for Maghribi, Arab and Turkish sociologists. In the absence of an autonomous local tradition of social analysis, it is hardly surprising that many Arab intellectuals have turned toward Marxism to provide a critique of the dominant Durkheimian and functionalist sociological tradition.

As a provisional classification, it is possible to identify three groups of radical/Marxist contributors to the analysis of the Middle East. There is an indigenous group of Arab Marxists who are influential in Tunisia and in Egypt at 'Ayn Shams University (Zghal and Karoui, 1973). There have also been notable contributions by Egyptian Marxists to the analysis of contemporary Egypt, such as Hussein (1973) and 'Abdel-Malek (1968). There is a second group of Marxist writers, in Israel, associated with the Israeli Socialist Organisation (Bober, 1972) which has produced important studies of the social structure of Israel and Zionism. Other radical critiques of Zionism have been presented by Davis, Mack and Yuval-Davis (1975), Ghilan (1974), by exiled Israeli Marxists such as the Israeli Revolutionary Action Committee Abroad (ISRACA) and by Uri Davis (1977). Finally, in this study of Marxist theories of the Middle East, I shall examine various contributions by European Marxists and radicals such as Chaliand (1972), Halliday (1974) and Rodinson (1973).

While there is in these Marxist analyses a basis for constructing a radical tradition of Marxist perspectives on the Middle East, Marxist theory suffers from difficulties which are not all that different from the ideological and theoretical difficulties of sociology in general. At one level, Marxism is no more an indigenous tradition in the Middle East than is Durkheimian sociology. Since Marx and Engels were primarily concerned with the theoretical analysis of the capitalist mode of production (hereafter, CMP) in order to understand the capitalist societies of Europe, the relevance of their theoretical work for the analysis of modes of production, the state and class struggles in the Middle East is by no means self evident. The work of conceptualising pre-capitalist modes of production, and the development of the CMP under colonialism, has barely begun so far as the Marxism of the Middle East is concerned, and

Marxist research is as underdeveloped as is the sociology of the Middle East as an area study. Furthermore, what Marx and Engels did say about Middle East societies has proved something of an ideological embarrassment for Marxists, since their observations have often been interpreted as a justification for colonialism. This can be made clear by a brief examination of Marx's book review (Easton and Guddat, 1967) of Bruno Bauer's *Die Judenfrage* and Engels' article in the *Northern Star* (Feuer, 1971) concerning the revolt of Abd el Kader against the French from 1832 to 1847.

Following a short period of political emancipation after the edict of 1812 the social and political position of Prussian Jews became increasingly anomalous after the Wars of Liberation. Liberals maintained that the 'Jewish Question' could be solved by granting equal rights to Jewish citizens, who would consequently abandon their peculiar customs and beliefs. On the other side, the conservatives were committed to the idea of the Christian state and opposed Jewish emancipation on the grounds that Jews could never be Prussianised. Bruno Bauer, who was the leading light in the Berlin Doctors' Club and a close associate of Marx in the 1830s, published a pamphlet on Jewish emancipation from the perspective of left Hegelianism. Bauer's argument was that full political emancipation could only be achieved when Christians and Jews abandoned the exclusive beliefs and practices which divided the two communities. However, the exclusiveness of Christianity was inherited from Judaism which, locked inside its ancient customs, represented a static, a-historical force in human progress. The dialectic of history required the Jews to abandon their narrow oriental faith if political progress in Prussia was to be achieved. Marx's review of Bauer's pamphlet appears to be based on a torrid anti-semitism (Bloom, 1942). This impression is, at least in part, created by the fact that Marx used his review as a pretext for a critique of commercial capitalism as a sordid, rapacious economic system. Marx played on the double meaning of *Judentum*—commerce and Jewry. The substance of his criticism was that Bauer had not gone far enough in attacking the limitations of political emancipation in the context of a Christian state. In Marx's view, political emancipation without social emancipation would still leave men in a condition of alienation within society. The real problem was the emancipation of men by the destruction of capitalism. Hence Marx's criticism of Bauer was a step in his transition from an idealist/Hegelian to a more materialist/historical view of alienation (Mészáros, 1970, pp. 70-92). His hostility to Moses Hess' Zionism was a function of Marx and Engels' notion that small nations could not provide an adequate context for capitalist development and proletarian revolution (Davis, 1965).

Whatever interpretation of Marx's views on Jewish emancipation is ultimately regarded as valid, there is undoubtedly a strong link between the Hegelian/Marxist opposition to Jewishness and Zionism in the 1840s and what was to emerge much later as the official line of the German Social Democratic Party (Meyer, 1939; Carlebach, 1977). The Hegelian opposition to Judaism as an exclusive, static phenomenon was replaced by Kautsky's view in *Rasse und Judentum* (1914) that Zionism was utopian romanticism and therefore reactionary. The wedge which was driven between Marxists and Zionists gave rise to an ironic ideological defence of the Jewish nationalist movement in terms of theoretical categories which claimed to be derived from Marxism. The main ingredients of the doctrine of 'proletarian Zionism' were assembled in the writing of the Russian Jew Ber Borochov (1881-1917). Every nation contains, according to Borochov (1937), a system of social stratification which is shaped like a pyramid: on top of a broad base of peasants and proletarians there are various layers of doctors, lawyers, intellectuals and employers. Jewry, however, is characterised by a deformed pyramid (the theory of the Inverted Pyramid) in which a narrow base of peasants and proletarians supports a wide band of professional groups. Borochov argued that Judaism could become socialist only after it had become proletarianised. The anomalies of the Jewish working class—its small size, its involvement in distribution and commerce rather than in productive industry—were the product of the anomalous historical role of Judaism as a nation without a homeland. Thus, the proletarianisation of Judaism also required a territorial solution, but this territorial dimension of Jewish socialism was not a case of colonialism since what he called 'the natives of Palestine' had no culture of their own and no national character. By means of this argument, Borochov was able to deduce Zionism, not from the interests of Jewry as a whole, but from the specific needs of the Jewish working class and to protect Zionism from any charge of colonial domination in Palestine. While Borochovism did not have any direct, permanent influence on political parties in Israel—apart from Po'aley Zion Smol—or on Jewish organisations in Europe, his general view of 'proletarian Zionism' and the notion that a territorial solution was the only method of destroying the traditional petty bourgeois character of Judaism have contributed significantly to various left wing Zionist interpretations of Jewish history (Arab League Office, n.d.). In Chapter 2 I shall attempt to show how elements of Borochovism play an important role in the Marxist apologetic for Zionism amongst contemporary Israeli socialists. The main point to establish here is that there is a theoretical continuity, of a basically Hegelian variety, which links together Bauer, Marx, Borochov and, in the modern period, Avineri (cf. Chapter 2). The common theme is that socialism is an historical necessity, which is achieved through various stages in history, and that the ultimate solution of 'the Jewish Question' is socialism via a prior process of proletarianisation. In short, Borochovism and related arguments rest upon teleological, historicist interpretations of Marxism, which are rooted in Hegelianism.

Similar Hegelian difficulties lie behind certain aspects of Marx and Engels' view of colonialism and capitalist expansion. In Chapter 2 I shall attempt to exorcise certain Hegelian and historicist versions of Marx's theory of colonialism in relation to Middle East development, but the nature of the problem may be indicated by reference to Engels' view of the French colonisation of Algeria. The revolt of Abd el Kader against the French forces was dismissed by Engels as the 'hopeless' struggle of 'the barbarian state of society', while the French conquest was welcomed as 'an important and fortunate fact for the progress of civilisation' (Feuer, 1971, p. 489). Engels' interpretation of these events is based on two major assumptions. The first is that the social formations of the Oriental world are stagnant and that capitalism has a historical role to play in smashing the pre-capitalist modes of production which dominate these formations. The second assumption is that 'small nations', or the revolts of minority groups, do not contribute to the development of capitalism as a system of global economic relationships. These two assumptions produced the political view that nationalist uprisings, popular protests and tribal opposition to the historical role of capitalism were necessarily reactionary. Thus Marx dismissed the Montenegrins as mere 'cattle robbers' while the Mexicans were *les derniers des hommes*. On the face of it, classical Marxism does not appear to be a promising source of revolutionary theory for movements of national liberation. In the Palestinian case, what sense can one make of the claim by the DPFLP that 'We are Marxist-Leninists' (Gerassi, 1971, p. 231)?

The burden of my argument so far has been that both conventional sociology and historicist Marxism are inadequate as perspectives for studying the Middle East. The sociology of the area is dominated by the French tradition of Durkheim and his school, or by conventional sociological approaches which are associated with such professional associations as the Middle East Studies Association or the British Society for Middle Eastern Studies. The major alternative to this sociological tradition is Marxism but the question then becomes, what type of Marxism? In this study of Marxist approaches to the Middle East, one aspect of my argument will be that, in order to establish an adequate basis for Marxist theory and analysis of Middle East social formations, there is a preliminary task of rejecting any teleological versions of Marxism which, for example, treat history as a series of necessary stages and thereby relegate the Middle East to a stage prior to 'real history'. This process of theoretical rejection will require some consideration of the epistemological claims of Louis Althusser (Althusser and Balibar, 1970) since Althusser provides us with a rationale for rejecting Marx and Engels' journalistic writing on colonialism as transitional analyses which were ultimately replaced by the scientific analysis of Marx's mature work. That Althusserian Marxism is not without its own difficulties (cf. Chapter 6) should not be unduly disconcerting; Althusser's critique of historicism is, at least, adequate to the task of undermining Hegelian Marxist interpretations of the Middle East.

Whilst Marxism and social science are underdeveloped in relation to the Middle East as an object for area studies, there exists an 'over-developed', luxurious tradition which has conventionally monopolised Middle East studies, namely the Orientalist study of art, literature, history and religion. These disciplines, their fundamental ideological assumptions and empiricist epistemology may be conveniently labelled 'Orientalism'. Orientalism takes as its object of study an entity referred to as 'Islamic civilisation' within which 'classical Islam' is the crucial feature. This 'civilisation' is treated as a bundle of elements of high culture, in particular religion, philosophy, architecture and poetry. The primary aim of Orientalism is to uncover the deep symbolic significance of Islamic cultural expression, of which the Arabic language is the primary vehicle. Hence research has been traditionally focused on the literary outpourings of the 'ruling institutions'—the *'ulemâ, Serây*, and the royal bureaucracy. Because of this concentration on the culture of the elite, Orientalism conceives politics as the internecine struggles of the royal family and history as the oscillation of dynasties. For urban geography, Orientalism substitutes the cartography of imperial cities, while political economy is replaced by the study of *wafq* legislation, the history of imperial finance, and numismatology.

The importance of Orientalism for this study of Marxism lies, not in its overt object of research, but in its covert assumptions and ideological underpinnings. There is, for example, the notion that, in contrast to Western society, Islamic civilisation is static and locked within its sacred customs, its formal moral code, and its religious law. The stationary quality of its culture is reinforced by the authoritarianism and despotism of its political system. Thus, as we shall discuss in Chapter 5, there is the perennial claim of Orientalist political studies that the Middle East has not been transformed by revolutions. If Orientalism does not assume that Islamic civilisation is static, then it claims, through the concept of 'classical Islam', that Islam is in slow, but inevitable decline. The most potent illustration of the decline thesis, in modern Orientalist scholar-ship, has been presented by G. E. von Grunebaum (1970); by founding his argument on the premise that 'classical Islam' is an ideal model constituted by the Islamic search for 'the correct life', the history of Islam must be a history of decline from the times of the Prophet. As David Waines aptly observes, 'the birth of Islam is also the genesis of its decline' (1976). The decline thesis is also to be found in most of the major Orientalist contributions to history (Gibb and Bowen, 1950; Lewis, 1964). While Islamic civilisation is either static or declining, Islam cannot produce adequate, scientific knowledge of itself, since the political conditions of Islamic societies preclude critical, autono-mous scholarship. Islam requires Western science to produce valid knowledge of the culture and social organisation of the Islamic world.

Orientalism is based on an epistomology which is essentialist, empiricist and historicist. The essentialist assumption is present in the notion that 'Islam' is a coherent, homogeneous, global entity, and also in the decline thesis where Islam is seen as declining because of some flaw in its essence. Social and political decline is a consequence of some historically ever-present element—authoritarianism, the lack of autonomous oppositional groups or laws, slavish adherence to formal custom or the failure of ruling institutions. This inner, flawed essence unfolds in history as a teleological process toward some final end-state which is the collapse of Islam and its civilisation. In this historicist approach, the dynamic history of Western civilisation, punctured by constant, progressive revolutions, is contrasted with the static history of Islam in which popular uprisings are merely an index of despotism and decay. In this kind of Orientalist analysis, issues of epistemology and method are avoided. Once the novice has mastered Arabic which the Orientalist, by professional agreement, recognises as 'a difficult language', there are few difficulties involved in research. The major problems of research for Orientalists are matters of philology, not epistemology.

The main features of Orientalism and its underlying epistemological assumptions have been documented by a number of critical observers (Laroui, 1973; Hodgson, 1974; Coury, 1975). What has been less commonly observed is the penetration of both sociology and Marxism by Orientalist categories and assumptions. In the case of sociology, there are important aspects of Orientalism in Max Weber's sociology of Islam (Turner, 1974a, 1974b). This can be seen, for example, in Weber's arguments about the decline of Islam, its despotic political structure and the absence of autonomous cities. Orientalist assumptions, as I shall indicate in Chapter 3, are present in various sociological positions which suggest that genuine social classes are absent in Islamic societies, along with social revolutions based on class conflict. By contrast, the Middle East is treated as a mosaic structure based primarily on ethnic diversity (Coon, 1951). However, Orientalism has also penetrated various Marxist contributions to Middle East studies. For example, the decline thesis pervades Perry Anderson's discussion of 'The House of Islam' in *Lineages of the Absolutist State* (1974) which is very dependent on Gibb and Bowen's Orientalist view of Ottoman institutions. Similarly, a false problem about the absence of capitalism in Islamic social formations inherited from Weberian sociology permits Orientalism to enter Maxime Rodinson's *Islam and Capitalism* (1974). There is, however, a more fundamental relationship between the Orientalist problematic and Marxism, namely, a correspondence between the historicism of the Orientalist approach and the historicism of Hegelian Marxism. Both forms of historicism are based on a model of history as a series of stages. For Hegelian Marxism it is the process of feudalism, capitalism and socialism, which in Orientalism takes the form of Genesis and Fall. There is also the ideal typical contrast, fundamental to both historicisms, between the dynamic, conscious West and the static, uncritical House of Islam. In Orientalism, the West is the recipient of Greek virtues (philosophy, democracy and individualism), while the Middle East is ossified by the particularity and exclusiveness of Judaism, on the one hand, and by the fanaticism and lethargy of fallen Islam, on the other.

The teleology of historical progress and the East-West contrast in both forms of historicism have their origins in Hegel's attempt to come to terms with the problem of Christianity in a society with an increasing division of labour. While an idealised Greek society provided Hegel with his model of harmonious, integrated communal existence, the rituals of Judaism (such as circumcision) provided the paradigm case of social alienation (Plant, 1973). Islam, which had once enjoyed a period of great creativity, had declined into 'Oriental ease and repose' (Hegel, 1956, p. 360). Christianity, influenced by Greek culture, and an offshoot of Judaism, presented an obvious problem which Hegel proposed to solve by providing a philosophical interpretation of Christianity in order to make it acceptable to modern man—the problem was, so to speak, to discover the rational kernel inside a mystified Christianity. We have already seen how this problem of human emancipation in the works of Hegel found its outlet in Bauer, Marx and Borochov. It is well known, of course, that Marx made a decisive break with this tradition in a series of critical works—the *Critique of Hegel's Philosophy of Right, Theses on Feuerbach* and *The German Ideology*. It is equally well known that these Hegelian themes of teleological self-awareness and reconciliation with society in which the social division of labour has been removed have what might be regarded as a theoretical 'bad habit' of reproducing themselves in Marxist theory. In recent times Lukács (1971) came to treat the proletarian class-for-itself as the subject of history and the embodiment of Truth. In this study of the Middle East I want to show that the Hegelian problematic finds its contemporary expression in the thesis that the social formations on which 'classical Islam' left an indelible mark have no 'real' class structure, no revolutions, and no history until they are incorporated within the global system of capitalist relations of production.

The controversy in sociology to which this study is addressed has three dimensions. First, it is important to demonstrate the philosophical limitations of Orientalism and to challenge its influence in contemporary sociology. However, since sociology itself is often regarded by Marxists as a form of ideological thought, the second objective must be to consider the ambiguous relationship between sociological and Marxist conceptions of Middle East social formations. Finally, because there is no such thing as a homogeneous tradition of Marxist analysis, this study is also concerned to attack Hegelian conceptions of Middle East issues from a standpoint which has been significantly influenced by Althusserian Marxism. In contemporary Marxism works of 'auto-critique' are virtually *de rigueur*. In saying that my intention is to challenge the influence of Orientalism I have not exempted my own publications on Islam (Turner, 1974a, 1974b) which bear the marks of Weberian Orientalism and in which I apparently succumbed 'congenitally and unwittingly' to the 'staples of the ideological market' (Al-Azmeh, 1976). This present study is, therefore, not only a critical analysis of sociological and Marxist approaches to Middle East studies, but in large measure a work of personal de-colonisation.

1

Marx on Colonialism and Capitalism

The contemporary sociology of development is heavily influenced, perhaps even dominated, by neo-Marxist theories of economic development and underdevelopment. Most sociologies of development hinge on the principal notion of capital accumulation at the centre of the world economy and socio-economic underdevelopment at the periphery. The theoretical debates about underdevelopment, dependency and the world division of labour have largely ousted the traditional problematic of 'mobilisation' in political science (Apter, 1965) and the conventional sociological concern for 'cultural factors' in the explanation of societal development (Peel, 1973). The traditional emphases on modernising the family or educational system as potential vehicles of Western values are now widely regarded as either naively ethnocentric or bourgeois and ideological. We may conveniently refer to the conventional sociological explanations of development as 'internalist theories' and contrast them with the 'externalist theories' which appear to be characteristic of modern Marxist approaches. My argument in this chapter is that, while Marxism has demolished much of the theoretical foundation on which internalist explanations were erected, an adequate Marxist alternative has not yet been securely established. Marx's theory of colonialism has proved to be inadequate in theoretical and empirical terms and this inadequacy is partly illustrated by the major disagreements within neo-Marxist theories of dependency and underdevelopment. Indeed, Marx's views on colonialism are secondary to the main focus of his theoretical work, namely, the crises of social formations in which the CMP is dominant. The problem facing anyone who wants an understanding of colonialism and neo-colonialism in the Middle East in Marxist terms is how to adapt the abstract categories of Marx's mature work in *Capital* to the concrete problems of Middle East social formations.

By an internalist argument, I mean a theory of development which treats the main problems of 'backward societies' as a question of certain characteristics internal to societies considered in isolation from any international societal context. Internalist research focuses on values, attitudes and motives as internal features of societies which either inhibit or promote modernisation. Associated with this approach to 'cultural factors' is a tendency to treat so-called problems of development as primarily features of individuals rather than of socio-economic structures. The assumption is that a society's capacity for change is retarded by certain archaic features of the beliefs or personalities of individuals—their traditionalist orientation to social problems, their magical beliefs or their inability to save for future growth. The absence of Weberian ingredients of growth—asceticism, rational law, bureaucracy, free labour—is an internal social virus which incapacitates the economic system. Another important dimension of internalist theory is that development is conceptualised in terms of a set of contrasts between dichotomous ideal types—*Gemeinschaft/Gesellschaft*, tradition/modernity, religious/secular. Alternatively development is treated as a process through a series of necessary stages—primitive, pre-modern, modern, post-industrial—which lead to an end-state society. The actual process of development takes the form of a gradual evolutionary unfolding of some inner essence (rationality) or the maturation of that essence (the modernisation process). The outcome of development is the achievement of a stationary end-state which is a faithful replica of the liberal democracies of Western capitalism. The most decisive example of an internalist explanation in sociology is Daniel Lerner's analysis of Middle East societies in *The Passing of Traditional Society* (1958), but internalism is not exclusively a sociological theory. David McClelland's *The Achieving Society* (1961) is a form of psychological theorising which has marked internalist assumptions. In the economics of development, the 'vicious circle of poverty' theory (Nurkse, 1953) and the principal assumptions about 'economic take-off' (Rostow, 1960) are examples of internalist theories. The solutions of 'backwardness' and the prescriptions for development which follow from these studies are also couched in terms of the internal changes of a society. Development can be brought about by a series of internal reforms directed at improving the education system, weakening the influence of traditional leaders, democratising the polity, or modernising the communication system.

By an externalist theory, I mean a theory of development which identifies the major problems facing a 'developing' society as external to the society itself, which is treated as a unit located within a structured international context. The primary dilemma of 'backward' societies is their dependency on the global structure of capitalist relations, their inability to fix favourable terms of trade, or their subservience to the interests of multinational corporations (hereafter, MNCs). Within this form of analysis the supposed characteristics of pre-modern individuals are causally irrelevant. The absence of modern personalities, institutions and values is a problem at the level of appearances which effectively masks genuine issues at the level of the world economy, for these apparently archaic institutions of a society are effects of causes which are external to that society. Furthermore, the simple dichotomies of traditional/modern society are rejected in favour of a far more differentiated picture of social change in terms of such concepts as developed, undeveloped, underdeveloped and dependent societies. The underdeveloped societies of today are not scaled-down models of what Western societies resembled in the seventeenth and eighteenth centuries; Britain may have been an undeveloped society but it was never underdeveloped by a network of exogenous forces. Once the CMP had been established in Britain, France, Germany and the United States as the dominant mode of production, the conditions for development in the rest of the world were decisively altered. The 'spontaneous' development of capitalism in Europe precluded similar capitalist development elsewhere by virtue of European capitalist expansion. Given the prior existence of a dominant set of global capitalist relations, externalist theories treat development as contingent upon a revolutionary restructuring of the relations of production within societies; and this class struggle can only be successful if an underdeveloped society can detach itself from the global system of capitalist production.

If the internalist perspective has some conception of the role of a world economic framework, it is based on the assumption that development is stimulated by the economic expansion of the centre of world capitalism. Capitalist growth in the United States, Japan and West Germany is held to result in a boom in commodity prices which is to the advantage of raw material exporters in the Third World (Hone, 1973). Externalist theories typically operate on the opposite assumption, namely, that the periphery can only develop when the centre is weak; international wars between capitalist societies and slumps in the economies of the capitalist centre are associated with rapid social and economic development at the periphery (Frank, 1969). The externalist prescriptions for development are in terms of class struggle against foreign and domestic agents of monopoly capitalism and detachment from the global system of capitalist exploitation rather than in terms of internal reforms of the education system, political representation and communications.

It is self-evident from my characterisation of these two approaches that internalist theories either implicitly or explicitly claim a Weberian parentage, whereas theorists within the externalist tradition trace their theoretical ancestry via Lenin, Bukharin, Hilferding and Luxemburg to Marx. Specifically, internalists are primarily concerned with the implications of Weber's studies of the institutional and motivational conditions for social change in the *Aufsätze zur Religionsoziologie* (1920-3), whereas externalist theories typically draw their inspiration from Marx's commentaries on British imperialism in his articles in the *New York Daily Tribune* or from Marx's analysis in *Capital* of the falling rate of profit and the role of capital exports for the crises of the CMP in Britain and the United States. The Weberian influence has been explicit in a number of studies by sociologists of Islam in relation to social development (Geertz, 1960; Bocock, 1971; Turner, 1974a), but potent, covert forms of Weberianism run through most internalist interpretations of the Middle East (Lerner, 1958; McClelland, 1963a, 1963b). In order to illustrate more precisely the nature of internalist explanations and Marxist/externalist objections to this approach, it will be salutary to examine *The Passing of Traditional Society*.

Lerner's theory is a typical end-state model of development. All societies start at the same developmental point of departure, namely, 'traditional society'. Such societies are based on restricted expectations, face-to-face systems of communication and a polity controlled by traditional authority figures such as tribal chiefs and religious leaders. At the other end of the development process we have what Lerner calls 'Participant Society' constituted by democratic participation, social welfare and consumerism. Expectations are wide and expansionary in societies where people are expected to make informed choices about political issues, commodities and social arrangements. The developmental process consists of a necessary sequence of phases. Increasing urbanisation is associated with increasing literacy, partly because mass education becomes economically feasible with increasing population density. Literacy is a basic necessity for achieving mass exposure to modern systems of impersonal communication in newspapers and television. In turn a system of mass communication makes possible wider involvement in politics (especially through voting) and also wider economic participation in the purchase of capitalist commodities. The 'secret' of the success of Western Participant Society was that the establishment of liberal democracy was achieved over many centuries of slow maturation so that contemporary political participation is founded on an efficient system of mass communications, industrial efficiency, and an adequate balance between town and country. By contrast, most of the societies of the Middle East are, according to Lerner, 'societies in a hurry'. Their developmental trajectory is off-course. Middle East governments have raised expectations too rapidly and they respond to economic failure by various defensive mechanisms—nationalism, xenophobia, Islamic fundamentalism and hatred of Western culture—which make recovery even more unlikely. Urbanisation, particularly in Egypt, has resulted in massive overcrowding and low levels of literacy. Authoritarian and extremist regimes in Egypt, Syria and Iran have curbed political choice and participation. The result is that Middle East societies generate frustrated middle classes which empathise with modern social objectives but are unable to realise their ambitions in any satisfactory manner. Lerner, however, recognises that the secularisation policy adopted by Turkey and the obvious commercialism of Lebanon have brought those two societies within reach of full modernisation. Lerner's scenario of political development in the Middle East has been supported by McClelland's view of Turkish entrepreneurs (1963c), by the contributions to Binder's *Politics in Lebanon* (1966) and by Inkeles and Smith (1974) on Israel.

Lerner's model, whereby in the context of urbanisation individuals achieve psychological mobility (empathy) as an effect of their geographical mobility, applies to 'virtually all modernizing societies on all continents of the world, regardless of variations in race, color, creed' (1958, p. 46). In the light of this claim, it is evident that Lerner's theory presents a unidimensional model of global development based on an ethnocentric view of Westernisation without any reference to the special problem of capitalist development at the periphery of global capitalism. Furthermore, the end-state of development is in fact competitive capitalism in which psychologically mobile consumers are systematically informed about their commodity choices via an efficient media service. Whereas Lerner's theory assumes a 'nightwatchman state', most societies that developed after Britain had gained a decisive capitalist advantage were forced to base their economic strategy on the interventionist state. One can suggest, in an obviously contentious way, that social formations like Germany and Italy were transformed from feudalism to *monopoly* capitalism rather than to competitive capitalism. Regardless of the European experience, it is certainly the case that development in the periphery cannot take place without massive state intervention (Wertheim, 1962). It is not clear, however, whether Lerner is presenting an ideal type of modernity or an empirical description since, in empirical terms, many examples could be presented of social formations which achieved capitalist development in a lop-sided, uneven process (Poulantzas, 1974) and which were far removed from the liberal/democratic model of a 'modern society'. Many other criticisms might be brought to bear against Lerner (Smith, 1971, pp. 89-105). Two further comments are important within the context of the critique of Orientalism. Lerner holds to the typical Orientalist view that traditional society is static—without history—and rejects nationalism as an ideological deviation which unhinges the development process.

While Marx's view of colonialism is usually called upon as the basis of a critique of conventional sociology of development, Marx's view of the impact of the CMP on colonial society as it is expressed in his articles in the *New York Daily Tribune* is often not very far removed from conventional 'bourgeois' sociology. There is, therefore, a permanent theoretical need for careful interpretation and systematic reinterpretation of Marxist theories of colonialism, underdevelopment and dependency. According to 'ideological readings' of Marx and Engels, their view of development appears to be a typically internalist analysis (cf. Chapter 2 of this study for further elaborations of this interpretation). From the perspective of the AMP, the problem of Asiatic development rests on a number of internal structural 'flaws'—self-sufficient village communities, the dominance of the state as the real landlord, the absence of classes, the ability of the social structure to absorb changes resulting from dynastic conquest. There is little in this basic formula to differentiate Marxism from the approach to Indian society which was taken by the English Utilitarians (Turner, 1974c). The historical stagnation of Asia is radically transformed by the introduction of dynamic elements of Western capitalism—private property in land, a railway system, a modernised army and communications system. The corollary of this position is that capitalist colonialism is a historical necessity and the brutality which accompanies colonial armies is ultimately justifiable. Only capitalism can destroy the economic basis of pre-capitalist modes which prevents Asia from entering a progressive historical path.

One possible defence of Marx and Engels runs as follows. The primary object of their mature analysis was the constitution of the CMP with special reference to the British social formation. Marx's 'theory' of colonialism and imperialism is secondary to this central focus and is introduced to account for certain aspects of those counteracting tendencies which serve to mitigate in the short term the crises of the CMP. In competitive capitalism, individual enterprises compete with each other for markets and profits. The basic mechanism of competition is to raise the productivity of labour by the introduction of processes of mechanisation which are associated with the increasing technical and social division of labour. This process has a number of contradictory consequences. The industrial reserve army of the unemployed constantly rises as workers are displaced by machinery. At the same time, employed workers are subject to various processes of de-skilling (Braverman, 1974) and to increased exploitation. The productivity of labour is associated with the need of capital to increase relative surplus-value and to reduce necessary labour-time. However, the replacement of men by machines results in a change in the ratio of constant capital ('dead labour') to variable capital ('living labour'). The organic composition of capital ($\frac{C}{V}$ or d) rises and while the absolute surplus-value (S) may rise the rate of profit falls, since the total capital employed includes constant and variable capital. Marx's law of the tendency of the rate of profit to fall may be expressed as follows:

$$r = \frac{S}{C + V}$$

$$= \frac{\dfrac{S}{V}}{\dfrac{C}{V} + 1}$$

$$= \frac{e}{d + 1}$$

where S = surplus-value, C = capital goods and materials, V = labour, S/V = the rate of surplus.

When S and V are equal and C is growing at a faster rate than either S or V, the value of the denominator increases more rapidly than the value of the numerator. With competition and increasing mechanisation, constant capital increases in relation to variable capital. Hence in capitalism the rate of profit has a tendency to fall as the organic composition of capital increases (Bullock and Yaffe, 1975). Further capital investment only results in a further reduction in the rate of profit.

There are two countervailing tendencies which can offset the fall in profitability without extending the market, namely, moderations in the rise of d and increases of e. That is, it is possible to reduce the costs of constant capital by capital-saving technology or it is possible to increase the rate of exploitation. Increases in exploitation, however, do not in the long run offset the rise in the organic composition of capital. The crisis of profitability in competitive capitalism results in increased state intervention at a variety of levels to maintain capitalist relations of production. Monopoly capitalism, however, also requires the export of capital to areas of the world where the organic composition of capital is lower in relation to the capitalist centre. In Lenin's view (1971), whereas in competitive capitalism imperialism takes the form of the export of finished goods, 'the highest stage of capitalism' involves the export of capital, first as portfolio capital and then as direct capital investment, in search of profits, which means in search of a lower organic composition of capital. However, as capitalist relations of production are successfully established, areas which previously enjoyed high profitability come to be characterised by an increasing ratio of constant to variable capital and profits fall. Imperialism thus constantly expands and intensifies as the crisis of capitalism is worked out on a global rather than local scale.

It appears, therefore, that in so far as Marx has a 'theory' of imperialism and colonialism, Marx regards capitalism as a system of production which must expand, with the result that it revolutionises and undermines pre-capitalist modes of production at the periphery of the capitalist world. In this rather technical and restricted sense it could be claimed that Marx thought that, other things being equal, the expansion of capitalist relations of production had 'progressive' effects. However, Marx had an equally significant view of the destructive and stunting effects of capitalist expansion. In the colonies, because of the abundance of land and the scarcity of labour, it proved difficult to establish capitalist relations of exploitation through the separation of the labourer from the means of production. The settler could not be readily coerced into selling his labour. Marx (1970, p. 716) observes that in the colonies 'the capitalist regime everywhere comes into collision with the resistance of the producer, who, as owner of his own conditions of labour, employs that labour to enrich himself, instead of the capitalist'. Capitalist development of colonies required an artificial rise in land prices by government purchase, or forced labour or slavery, in order to provide an adequate supply of landless wage labourers. In his discussion of the theoretical errors involved in equating 'mode of production' and 'relations of exploitation', Jairus Banaji (n.d.) shows that the extension of new relations of production based on capital into previously non-capitalist areas actually intensifies and reproduces 'backward' forms of exploitation (slavery and serfdom). In the colonies, the introduction or intensification of pre-capitalist forms of exploitation, especially slave labour, is a characteristic effect of capitalism. There is no automatic transformation of labour-power into a commodity operating within a 'free' labour market with the development of capitalist economies. The production of cotton in the slave South is the most obvious illustration of this paradoxical development. With respect to the classical debate about the necessity of colonialism/imperialism as a progressive historical force it must be said that capitalism may actually contribute, in terms of 'relations of exploitation', to the development of archaic modes of labour organisation.

Marx's commentaries on Ireland, especially in *Capital*, Vol. I, provide a clear illustration of his views on the destructive consequences of capitalist colonialism. In Ireland, landlords and capitalists joined together to exploit an indigenous population with the result that Ireland 'has been stunted in its development by the English invasion and thrown centuries back' (Marx and Engels, 1968, p. 319). This view of colonialism provided the theoretical germ for the view that pressure from white settlers is the primary cause of continued colonial expansion as a method of subjugating indigenous labour rather than the pressure from invest-ment imperialism (Emmanuel, 1972). It may be suggested that Marx's view of the 'stunting' effect of colonial invasions has some connections with later neo-Marxist conceptions of underdevelopment (Foster-Carter, 1974). However, despite these features of Marx's perspective, in which the retarding consequences of capitalist expansion are considered, his primary view is clearly that the CMP destroys pre-capitalist modes and thereby lays the foundations for historically progressive developments. In general the CMP has both conservation and dissolution effects on pre-capitalist modes of production (Poulantzas, 1975a), but in his commen-taries on colonialism Marx thought that the dissolution effects would predominate and liquidate the archaic institutions of undeveloped social formations.

Given the level of technological development and industrial organisa-tion at the beginning of the twentieth century, capital accumulation on a global scale could have developed by either capital-widening or capital-deepening (Hymer, 1972). In the first, capital-widening, economic development would have involved the global expansion of mass production systems making consumer goods available on a wide basis. In the second option, capital is deepened within existing industrial societies and continuous innovation in commodities is focused on a restricted market. The consequence of capital-deepening is the production of a permanent dualism in the world economy between a restricted high-wage, capital-intensive sector in advanced societies and an extensive low-wage, low-productivity sector in the underdeveloped, dependent world (Barratt Brown, 1974). Marx's primary standpoint was that, despite certain stunting and regressive effects, in the long term capital would expand by widening and that any dualistic features at the global level would be eradicated by revolutionary class struggle within the capitalist centre and in the colonial periphery. In fact, capitalist global development has taken both a different and a more complex course than Marx's premises suggest.

In historical terms, capital investment has not been directed to countries with a labour surplus but to those with a labour shortage, so that indentured labour or slave labour has to be imported to provide an adequate labour supply. Where capital was invested or finished commodities found a colonial market, the result was that potential industrial capital in the colony was destroyed and replaced by comprador merchant capital whose agents served the interests of foreign capital in alliance with indebted feudal landlords (Kay, 1975). Any subsequent industrialisation is highly dependent upon financial aid which is controlled and organised by foreign sources. In the period since the Second World War, the international economy has been restructured in terms of the global control exercised by MNCs most of which are American based. With the development of joint financial ventures, however, most subsidiaries receive only a small fraction of their investment requirements direct from the parent corporation. The growth of local capital sources has produced a net *outflow* of capital from underdeveloped to developed societies through various channels of capital repatriation. Such investment strategies appear to be moving away from traditional exploitation of mining and plantations to manufacturing, but often this involves a dependent society producing components of manufactured goods which are assembled elsewhere. Despite arguments to the effect that the boom in commodity prices has fundamentally changed the structure of the international economy (Warren, 1973), the Third World has been downgraded as a market, because the bulk of international trade is between advanced capitalist societies through the medium of the MNCs (Tugendhat, 1973). The effect on underdeveloped societies of these reorganisations of the world economy is to produce a new dualism, not between agrarian feudalism and industrial capitalism, but between 'a high profit/high wage international oligopolistic capitalist sector and a low profit/low wage competitive local capitalist sector' (Barratt Brown, 1974, p. 276). In order to bring these developments within its theoretical framework it will be necessary for Marxist analysis to change its focus from the theory of underdevelopment to that of dependent development, in order to provide explanations which differentiate between dependent poor societies (India) and dependent rich societies (Canada). The main lesson, however, to be drawn from these recent debates in Marxist theory of capital accumulation is that unidimensional concepts of 'progress' or 'underdevelopment' are theoretically inadequate.

In Chapter 2 I shall approach the problem of historicism in Marx's treatment of colonialism by concentrating on the use of the AMP in the analysis of the Middle East. Prior to that discussion, however, it is important to consider briefly the conservation and dissolution effects of the CMP on Middle East social formations through the process of imperialism and colonialism. While each society within the Middle East has undergone a unique development process depending on its own internal structure and its method of incorporation within the world division of labour, the Middle East has typically been subject to what Marxists have referred to as the 'law of combined and unequal development' (Dos Santos, 1970). Development has been unequal in that some sectors of the economy and social formation develop at the expense of other sectors; it is combined because it involves a combination of inequalities which are intensified and systematically structured by the transfer of resources from underdeveloped to advanced industrial societies (Halliday, 1974, p. 17). These features of combined and unequal development may be illustrated by reference to three societies—Lebanon, Egypt and Algeria—which were prized out of the disintegrating Ottoman imperial orbit in the nineteenth century by French and British capital.

Before the French and British mandates of 1920, the Lebanese social formation was subject to two contradictory processes: one involving the destruction of the traditional 'feudalised' Ottoman system under the impact of European trade and Lebanese merchant capital, and the other promoting the conservation of dependent mercantile capitalism at the expense of industrial capital (Saba, 1976). In the nineteenth century, grain production for export increased considerably in response to European demand in the aftermath of the Napoleonic wars. There was almost simultaneously a progressive extension of the cultivation of the mulberry tree in response to the demand from Egypt for raw silk following the reforms of Muhammad Ali Pasha (Holt, 1966). This export trade stimulated handicraft production (of silk and cotton cloth), money transactions, and merchant capital, which began to penetrate the peasant barter economy. In social class terms, a middle peasantry developed with the *métayage* system of land cultivation alongside an artisan class which was engaged in weaving for export. These embryonic instances of production for the market were set within the context of an economy in which the mass of the peasantry was bound by feudal dependence to sheikhs and emirs. However, with the rapid increase of trade under merchant capital between 1827 and 1862, the dominant role of the feudal landlords was challenged by the development of powerful merchant capitalists centred in Beirut. The traditional power of feudal lords was further weakened during the Egyptian occupation by the armies of Ibrahim Pasha from 1832 to 1840 (Hourani, 1946). While the Egyptian administration raised taxes, feudal lords were deprived of customary rights of tax extraction.

By the middle of the nineteenth century, the inflow of British textiles seriously undermined local cloth manufacture in Lebanon and Syria (Smilianskaya, 1966). The resulting unemployment, loss of revenue, increasing exploitation of the peasantry, and indebtedness of feudal landlords constituted a general crisis of the 'feudal' economy. The surplus peasant labour force was compelled to migrate, and as the traditional landlord became increasingly dependent on Beirut merchants, the feudal lord was replaced by merchants and usurers who were not restrained by customary obligations toward the peasantry (Wolf, 1971a, 1971b). Under conditions of increasing economic pressure, peasant rebellions and inter-confessional tensions became commonplace (Johnson, 1975). Because of the political uncertainty and the difference in investment returns, the surplus which was extracted from agriculture and from trade was not invested in industrial capital or in agricultural development. Secure investment was sought in trade and usury, or in urban property such as warehouses and shops to rent. The characteristic features of the Lebanese social structure in the twentieth century were established by these nineteenth century developments. The Lebanese social formation is defined by a precocious growth of merchant capital and its attendant financial apparatus at the expense of industrial capital. While there was virtually no urban working class in manufacturing industry, the peasantry was under pressure to migrate from the archaic agricultural sector to find employment abroad. The dominant mercantile bourgeoisie was positively encouraged by government policy, which included abolition of the exchange control, establishment of a free gold market, low tariffs and a bank secrecy law. Various 'historical accidents' also contributed to the development of Beirut as the financial centre of the Middle East; in particular the Arab boycott of Israel meant that Beirut rather than Tel Aviv and Haifa became the hub of Arab bank deposits for oil, trade and tourism. Finally, as in most post-colonial social formations, the service sector dominates both agriculture and industry. In 1970 services provided 68 per cent of GNP in Lebanon while industry accounted for 22 per cent leaving agriculture with a mere 10 per cent.

A similar pattern of unequal and combined development is to be found in the political economy of Egypt and Algeria. The main features of the 'lop-sided development' of modern Egypt are well known (Issawi, 1963; Owen, 1969; Radwan, 1974). The eventual failure of Muhammad Ali

Pasha's reform programme in industry and agriculture (Dodwell, 1967) forced the Egyptian economy into international dependency as a mono-crop exporting agriculture. While irrigated land was extended by 20 per cent for cotton production, food production failed to keep up with the growth in population. Almost half of the value of exports in the nineteenth century was allocated to the payment of foreign bond-holders. At the same time, the value of cotton as an export crop declined on the world market and also suffered from competition from American cotton and synthetic fibres. With the extension of land given over to cotton production, Egypt ceased to be a wheat-exporting economy and was forced to import increasing amounts of wheat. The surplus from cotton exports was either repatriated to foreign interests or reinvested in cotton production or diverted to the service sector such as banking and insurance. Indigenous handicrafts were undermined by foreign imports, and manufacturing industry, apart from those technical processes associated with the treatment of the export crop, was starved of invest-ment by foreign capitalists and by Egyptian landlords whose main interest lay in keeping Egypt as 'the cotton farm' of Europe.

With the Great Depression and the emergence of a strong nationalist movement, various attempts were made in the thirties to switch from cotton export to import-substitution industrialisation and tariff protec-tion as an answer to the crisis in agriculture. The politics of the interwar period represent a largely unresolved conflict between three sections of the dominant class—the aristocracy of predominantly Turkish origin centred on the Palace, the nationalist bourgeoisie of Egyptian origin, and finally a modernist bourgeoisie who were somewhat separate from the traditional rural ruling class (Hussein, 1973). This intra-class struggle was not resolved in such a manner as to direct the Egyptian economy into a decisive phase of industrialisation. Similar problems dogged the Nasser regime despite attempts at land reform, agrarian reform, industrialisa-tion and increased social overhead capital. The Nasser regime involved a change in the personnel of the bourgeois class rather than its overthrow and thereby represented an important continuity with the past (Mansfield, 1969). Nasser's land reforms broke the power of the old aristocracy without solving the basic problems of agricultural producti-vity; the nationalisation policy did not extend to the land. The public sector operated according to the profit criteria of the market. Egypt has developed a post-colonial state of classic proportions (Alavi, 1972) so that in the 1960s manufacturing accounted for 10 per cent, agriculture for 54 per cent and services for 20 per cent of the labour force ('Abdel-Malek, 1964). Egypt's traditional indebtedness and dependence on foreign finance has increased considerably in the 1970s. With exports falling well behind imports, a trade deficit of E£192 million in 1972 rose to E£1,361 million in 1975, while in the same period debt servicing rose from E£353 to E£1,235 million (Aulas, 1976). President Sadat's 'open door' policy of liberalising the economy by encouraging the private sector and foreign investment appears to be increasing the trade deficit by opening Egypt to the importation of luxury goods rather than stimulating private investment in manufacture and construction.

Unlike the forms of indirect, mandatory control of Lebanon and Egypt through an imperial administration, Algeria was forcibly colonised from 1840 onwards with devastating effects on its pre-colonial social structure (Gallissot, 1975). Irrigated, productive land within the public domain (*beylik* property) and lands traditionally allocated to religious or charitable ends (*habous* or *waqf* property) were annexed. A variety of restrictions were placed on the use of tribal, communal lands (*bled el'arsh*) and the property of rebel tribes was confiscated. Private or family land (*melk*) which was traditionally bound by customary rights (such as indivision) and over which the sovereign had ultimate title, was converted by colonial legislation into individual private property. This legal conversion of *melk* into a commodity for the market destroyed traditional customs which gave the peasant some degree of economic security in the pre-colonial system and transferred land via purely economic mechanisms into the hands of colons (Wolf, 1971a, 1971b). By these means, the French colonate gained the lion's share of the best cultivated land in the plains and coastal regions, which had the effect of destroying the balance between cultivators and nomads and creating massive rural unemployment. Demographic changes also forced male workers into the larger towns and eventually into France. The population of Algeria jumped from approximately 2.5 million in 1840 to 5.5 million in 1910. Urbanisation and sedentarisation produced rapid rural migration, a badly distributed population, and rural overpopulation especially in the Kabylia which achieved a population density of some 150 inhabitants per square kilometre.

While the European colons revolutionised the methods of agricultural production, the Muslim traditional agricultural economy stagnated and by the 1930s the rate of agricultural growth fell below the rate of population growth. In 1953, the European settlers produced some 65 per cent of the total agricultural product. Agriculture is dominated by colonial viticulture which prior to independence represented 35 per cent of the gross vegetable output and over half of Algeria's exports to France. The acreage set aside for vineyards doubled in the first half of the twentieth century with a consequent diminution of food crops and sheep pasturage. This development of a cash crop for export produced a characteristic dual economy: an export-oriented European sector versus a subsistence cereal-livestock sector based on an underdeveloped hinterland (Murray and Wengraf, 1963). The European sector contributed to the decline of the traditional sharecropping system and converted the rural peasantry into seasonal wage labourers. The structure of the economy is clearly reproduced in social class structure and in terms of sectors. The indigenous artisan class declined or stagnated, but their functions in the economy were not acquired by manufacturing industry which did not develop significantly under colonial conditions. In 1955, large-scale industry accounted for less than 8 per cent of the gross domestic output and important sectors of light industry never developed (Amin, 1970). It is typical of colonial agrarian capitalism that, apart from investment in mining and construction, the system requires a top-heavy administrative class to manage the service sector. Out of a European work force of 300,000, administration counted for 50,000 workers, while services represented 160,000 employees. Thus, in 1954, transport, commerce and services amounted to 39 per cent of the gross domestic product.

After the Second World War the Algerian economy began to suffer from a severe balance of payments deficit resulting from a rapid growth of imports. While Algerian exports continued to expand (especially with the increasing importance of oil exports), there was an inflow of public capital in the context of the French economic plan. However, a significant factor in Algeria's financial difficulties arose from the growth in public expenditure on the military and other aspects of internal security. In 1955, when public expenditure amounted to around 246,000 million francs, the expenditure on police, administration of justice, security and military expenses was over 70,000 million francs. Despite major increases in taxation and in the value of exports, the expansion of expenditure in capital resources after 1947 meant that Algeria became permanently dependent on foreign investment and foreign loans. The post-colonial government inherited an unbalanced socio-economic structure with the additional difficulty of a short-term shortage of skilled and professional manpower following the exodus of the French colonial middle class. There was also a massive transfer of capital from Algeria to France between 1960 and 1962 as the revolutionary conflict began to turn against France. The vulnerability of independent Algeria was further underscored by its near complete dependence on France as the importer of Algerian wine, oil, vegetables and minerals (Humbaraci, 1966).

These three colonial histories illustrate a common pattern of unequal and combined development in a context of international dependency. The imperialism of foreign trade and capital investment resulted in the destruction of indigenous petty commodity production and small industrial capital. The growth in the population in the nineteenth century was accompanied by a decline in the food supply as each society became dependent on mono-crop export agriculture—silk, cotton or wine. This situation produced the typical profile of an underdeveloped society which combines rural overpopulation, urban unemployment, emigration and sedentarisation of pastoral nomads. While the manufacturing sector does begin to expand despite declining investment efficiency, traditional agriculture stagnates. In these societies the expansion of capital is associated with archaic forms of labour organisation and exploitation.

Increasing military, security and commercial needs are associated with a precocious explosion of the service sector in a social formation where the various indigenous and compradorial classes are orchestrated by a massive, post-colonial state apparatus.

This brief outline of dependency within the Middle East serves to underline the problems that are associated with any interpretation of Marx which focuses on the supposedly progressive and dynamic aspects of the expansion of capital. It is possible from a close scrutiny of Marx's writing on India and Ireland to maintain that Marx had an alternative perspective on colonialism which took notice of its stunting, retarding effects. However, what Marx did not possess was a notion that 'capitalism as a whole should be viewed, not as a process or pattern of processes, but as a *relation* of unequal partners of whom one developed at the expense of the other' (Foster-Carter, 1974, p. 70). In offering this preliminary discussion, I have deliberately referred to Marx's 'writing', 'commentaries' and 'observations' on colonialism rather than to Marx's 'theory' of colonial underdevelopment and dependency. This terminology results from the fact that, while Marx generated a theory of the crises of the CMP, he did not possess a fully fledged, coherent theory of non-European social formations—their histories, structures and contradictions. This assertion, of course, rests upon certain theoretical decisions regarding the validity of Marx's observations on 'Asiatic society', namely, the AMP. In the following chapter, I shall examine the use of the concept of an Asiatic mode in explaining the imputed backwardness of Arab society in relation to the capitalist development of Israel.

2

Marxist Theories of the Middle East

The difficulties of formulating a 'correct' attitude towards Israel and Zionism have long daunted socialists in Europe and North America. The Old Left had traditionally identified with Israel as a socialist democracy surrounded by feudal Arab potentates who had the backing of both reactionary European conservatives and the oil companies of monopoly capitalism (Jones, 1970). The annexation of Arab territories following the Sinai campaign of 1956, the Six Days' War and the Yom Kippur War produced a change of perspective among the New Left which viewed the Palestinians as a homeless people caught between Israel as an imperialist outpost and feudal pro-British states such as Jordan. The events of 'Black September', the urban development of Jerusalem, Israeli involvement in the Lebanese civil war and reports of systematic torture of Arabs in Israel all tended to confirm and reinforce left-wing criticism of Israeli policy and Zionist ideology (Cooley, 1973; Langer, 1975). Of course, socialist critiques of Israel have varied considerably in terms of the degree to which they reject the Israeli state and its dominant Zionist ideology (Farsoun *et al.*, 1974). The enormous variety of New Left perspectives on the Middle East crisis is further complicated by the development of dissent and opposition within Israel itself (Nahas, 1976; Glass, 1976). In the light of this political and theoretical diversity, it is pertinent to consider Shlomo Avineri's Marxist perspective on Israel and the Middle East, since Avineri is both a representative of 'humanist Marxism' which has been favoured by certain groups within the New Left and an advocate of Israeli socialism.

As against the Althusserians, Avineri regards Marx's social philosophy as a relatively homogeneous and continuous theoretical production. Marx's *Paris Manuscripts, The Communist Manifesto*, the journalism, and *Capital* enjoy a similar analytic value and theoretical integrity. In addition, Avineri attempts to emphasise the massive continuity in terms of analytical themes and objects of theoretical inquiry between Hegel and Marx. The themes of alienation, objectification and reification provide the primary focus which accounts for the seamless development in Marx's theory of social formations and their dialectical histories, and illustrates the continuity between Hegel and Marx. The basic premise is that man as a social being creates a socio-cultural world and shapes the natural environment through human labour. At the same time, this human reality is experienced as an objective, natural phenomenon which stands outside and in opposition to man. History is the dialectic between subject and object, between man as a subjective agent and the social world as objective datum. This historical process is punctuated by an evolution of human consciousness about the world so that man constantly transcends the limitations of nature and society (*Aufhebung*). At the core of Marx there exists the theoretical apparatus of Hegel's concepts of Spirit and History whereby 'the dialectics of *Aufhebung* ensures a progressive and expanding continuum of human capacity to experience and explain the world, not because the world is a given objective datum, but, on the contrary, because it is consciously created by man' (Avineri, 1968b, p. 84).

According to Avineri's interpretation of Marx, the irony of capitalism is that while it represents, through the separation of workers from the means of production and the dominance of the 'cash nexus', a profound form of human alienation, it also contains within itself the potential for socialist development and de-alienation of human existence. Capitalism destroys the illusions and mystifications of feudalism, replacing the personal dependency between lord and serf by the impersonalism of labour as a commodity. Whereas in pre-capitalist social formations human relationships are arbitrary and particularistic, capitalism is abstract, impersonal and universalistic. Within the European context, bourgeois capitalism 'has put an end to all feudal, patriarchal, idyllic relations. It has pitilessly torn asunder the motley feudal ties that bound man to his "natural superiors", and has left remaining no other nexus between man and man than naked self-interest, than callous "cash payment"' (Marx and Engels, n.d., p. 52). The expansion of capitalism results in the export of social relations based upon this universalism, so that the particularism of local tribes, of small nations, and the 'idiocy of rural life' are liquidated by the impact of capitalist relations of production and capitalist commodities. This theme in Marx which treats history as a dialectic between particularism and universalism is taken from Hegel's philosophy of history and developed with special reference to the revolutionary role of the proletariat as a 'universal class' (Avineri, 1967).

This imputed Hegelianism of Marx's theory of capitalism is brought out with special emphasis in Avineri's treatment of colonial capitalism and the AMP. 'Capitalist society is universalistic in its urges, and will not be able to change internally unless it encompasses the whole world' (Avineri, 1968a). Capitalism is propelled by the conflict between the proletariat as a general, universalistic class and the bourgeoisie as the defender of sectional, particularistic interests. By contrast, social formations which are dominated by the AMP have no internal class conflicts and are consequently trapped within a static social context. Because in the AMP the state is 'the real landlord' (Marx and Engels, 1972, p. 79), there is no private property in land and no property-owning class. The social system thereby lacks a basic ingredient of social change, namely, class struggle between landlords and an exploited peasantry. In the *Communist Manifesto*, Marx and Engels had established the basic principle of their view of history in which all real social change is the effect of class struggle. Since Asia prior to colonial penetration had no social classes, it had no real history apart from the circulation of dynasties. For example, 'Indian society has no history at all, at least no known history' (Marx and Engels, 1972, p. 81). What passes for the 'history of India' is merely the chronicle of successive conquests which replaced the royal household but preserved the basic economic conditions that supported India's social stationariness. The historic role of British capitalism in India was to destroy the dominance of the AMP by creating private property in land and by demolishing the traditional village system. Avineri reminds us that by treating Asian countries as Oriental Despotisms without history, Marx is repeating an interpretation of the basic difference between Oriental and Occidental social structures which derives from Hegelian philosophy. The history of the Oriental states 'is, for the most part, really *unhistorical*, for it is only the repetition of the same majestic ruin' (Hegel, 1956, p. 106).

Avineri is thus committed to the classical Hegelian-Marxist view of the 'necessity' of imperialism as the catalyst of world history (Bukharin, 1972, ch. 12). The importation of capitalist relations of production is the only condition by which social formations based on the AMP can be revolutionised and brought into world history. The corollary of this view is that the greater the intensity of capitalist colonialism, the greater the potential for radical change in Asia and the Middle East. Thus 'the more direct the European control of any society in Asia, the greater the chances for the overhauling of its structure and its ultimate incorporation into bourgeois, and hence later into socialist, society' (Avineri, 1968a, p. 18). This perspective provides the basis for Avineri's view of the historical conditions of Arab backwardness and the progressive nature of Israeli capitalism. Apart from the obvious case of Algeria, most Middle East societies experienced European imperialism in the form of indirect rule. 'Whether it was called protectorate or mandate, the system ensured the overall paramountcy of the Western power without involving it in direct administration—without, therefore, basically affecting the socio-economic infrastructure of Arab society' (Avineri, 1972, p. 301). Instead of destroying the old social structure of Arab society, indirect colonialism merely reproduced the existing militarism and backwardness of the ruling elites. The military societies of the modern Middle East are thus the direct descendants in terms of values and social role of the Turks, Seljuks and Mamluks. The European powers provided modern military technology without revolutionising the basic social structure which is stagnant and archaic.

In order to characterise Israeli society and Zionist socialism, Avineri combines Ber Borochov's territorial solution of the 'Jewish problem' with Hegel's view of the march of history. The tragedy of the Israeli-Arab confrontation is that it represents a struggle between two national-ist social movements in which only Jewish nationalism is genuinely radical and progressive. The Jewish national movement is based on a political struggle for self-determination and a social revolution of Jewish society, whereas the Arabic national movement has 'remained almost exclusively political—an Arab social revolution, indeed, has yet to be undertaken' (Avineri, 1970, p. 34). This double revolution, political and social, gave Israel its transformative, progressive features. Following Borochov's account of the inverted pyramid, Avineri argues that the formation of a national homeland in Palestine revolutionised the tradi-tional social structure of the Diaspora by destroying its petty bourgeois characteristics. The Jewish migration and settlement of Palestine was 'the only intentionally downwardly mobile social movement ever experienced in the history of immigration' (Avineri, 1970, p. 35). Migration transformed the Diaspora petty bourgeoisie into an Israeli working class. Israeli colonisation was unlike the typical white colonisa-tion of South Africa or Algeria because Zionism rejected the exploitation of cheap Arab labour and preached the values of self-reliance and labour.

If the indirect imperialism of European capitalism reproduced the pre-colonial values and structure of Egypt and Syria, the direct colonisation of Israel in Palestine has started the process of modernisation on the West Bank and Gaza Strip. The Arabs in Israel and occupied territories are being slowly but irrevocably transformed from a backward peasantry into an urban working class. The Israeli mass media are a significant channel for the exposure of Arabs to realistic and informed analysis of political and social issues. Arab municipal authorities enjoy a consider-able degree of political autonomy which provides Arabs with a basic experience of political democratisation in the context of Israeli society with its 'social cohesion, basic egalitarianism, determination and relative openness' (Avineri, 1971, p. xix). Through the provision of a modern economic infrastructure, a democratic political apparatus and urban facilities, Israel has acted as the 'inadvertent midwife' of a profound social and economic revolution in Arab Palestine (Shaicovitch, 1973). Israeli occupation has cut the link between Arabs in Israel and the archaic ruling classes of surrounding Arab states and thereby provided the necessary conditions for Arab modernisation.

Avineri's view of Marx's theory of colonialism can be challenged on a variety of grounds—for inadequately discussing the range and variety of Marx's commentaries on colonialism, for exaggerating Marx's dependence on Hegel, for failing to take note of the 'stunting effect' of direct colonialism, for his inflated views on Israeli modernisation (Turner, 1976). However, rather than attack Avineri's position on all fronts, the most economical approach is to consider the empirical validity of Avineri's discussion of the modernisation of Arabs in Israel and then to raise the problem of the theoretical adequacy of the concept of the AMP. While Avineri regards the effects of Israeli colonial capitalism as unambiguously positive in that it starts the painful process of modernisation, the actual development of the Arabic socio-economic structure illustrates a much more complex process of combined and unequal development (Trotsky, 1932, Vol. 1).

In the aftermath of the Six Days' War, Israeli leaders made two crucial decisions concerning the future economic role of the West Bank and Gaza in relation to the Israeli economy. The first was to allow some limited use of Arab labour from the territories within the Israeli economy. As the economy moved out of the recession of 1966-7, the level of unemployment in Israel fell from 10 per cent in 1967 to less than 3 per cent in 1973. The economic boom produced a scarcity in the labour market so that the employment of Arab labour increased significantly. The number of Arabs from the territories working in Israel jumped from 9,000 in 1969 to 70,000 in 1974. The second decision was to open the Arab market in the territories to Israeli commodities and to permit the import of food products from the territories. Within this economic relationship, Israel was clearly the dominant partner. By the early 1960s, construction and industry amounted to 33 per cent of Israel's GNP while agriculture had fallen to a mere 7 per cent. By contrast in the late 1960s agriculture in the territories contributed over 37 per cent of GNP while industry and construction barely achieved 13 per cent. The relationship between Israel and the territories was, therefore, typical of dependent development within the context of a dual economy. Israel is an advanced capitalist society characterised by a high wage, capital-intensive, exporting economy, while the territories are underdeveloped regions with a labour surplus. However, unlike other dependent regions, the territories have not been in a position to utilise traditional defensive measures such as tariffs and exchange rate adjustments (Arkadie, 1977). In addition, the high tariff barriers which protect the Israeli economy force Arab consumers in the territories to purchase foreign goods at high prices or to buy them from expensive Israeli suppliers. In this context of unequal exchange, the territories have been unable to retain Arab labour which is drawn into the Israeli labour market, while its own manufacturing industry has stagnated under the impact of Israeli goods. Other sectors—such as the West Bank tourist trade—have been lost to the Israeli economy, while other long-term opportunities such as exports to other economies have been halted in the post-1967 period.

These changes in the economic structure of the West Bank and Gaza

Strip are clearly demonstrated in the class structure of the dependent territories. The central feature of the changing class structure of the Palestine Arabs is the transformation of the peasantry into a rural proletariat of migrant and seasonal wage labourers (Zureik, 1976). While the Jewish settlers, contrary to the ideological theme of working the land, have gone to urban areas, the Arabs have been confined to the rural hinterland. The percentage of Jews in urban settlements has risen from 74 per cent in 1931 to over 90 per cent in 1974, while in 1963 over 75 per cent of the Arabs in Israel were rural (Ben-Porath, 1966; Harari, 1974). In 1972, agricultural occupations accounted for 20 per cent of the employed Arabs in Israel, but only 7 per cent of all employed Jews were in agricultural occupations. The pattern of Arab employment is, however, changing rapidly with a significant increase in the number of Arabs working as unskilled labour in the construction and mining industries. In 1972, over 26 per cent of all employed Arabs were engaged in construction and mining. Because of the strong pull from the Israeli labour market, all forms of employment in the territories have declined since 1967. The number of Arabs employed in West Bank agriculture declined from 10,400 in 1969 to 3,900 in 1973. In the same period, construction workers in the territories declined from 11,700 to 5,800.

The dominant effect, therefore, of the Israeli occupation has been to convert the Arabs into a migrant labour force which is concentrated in unskilled occupations in agriculture and construction industries. The other effect on the agrarian social structure has been the sedentarisation of the Bedouin tribes. It is possible to distinguish between forced sedentarisation which involves the intervention of the state to settle nomads for reasons of political security or to develop the land and spontaneous sedentarisation which takes place, for example, with the increasing prosperity of a particular nomadic family (Barth, 1964). The Bedouin in the north of Israel around the hills of Galilee who number about 8,000 persons are fully settled. The nomads of the Negev at the end of the mandatory period amounted to 65-90,000, but following the conflict of 1948 they have dispersed, leaving an estimated 14,000 Bedouins who are confined to a reservation east of Beersheba. Nomadic migrations within the reservation are limited and these tribesmen are consequently firmly set on the process of sedentarisation (Muhsam, 1959). Sedentarisation is taking place partly because of population pressure on the limited resources of the reservation and partly as a consequence of Israeli policy requirements for greater security within the area. Settled Bedouin are being converted into seasonal wage labourers on Israeli citrus orchards and cotton plantations. Despite elementary provision of amenities, the Israeli policy toward the Bedouin amounts to forced sedentarisation; 'no other Middle Eastern country, except Turkey, has treated its nomads so badly, and developments are reminiscent of American Indian reservations' (George, 1973).

The proletarianisation of the peasantry and sedentarisation of the Bedouin have to be set in a context of Israeli colonisation of the territories and Arab migration and expulsion. Without counting the refugees who fled after the Six Days' War, between 132,000 and 141,000 people emigrated from the West Bank and Gaza. The majority of those who are forced to leave or emigrate voluntarily are young, male, skilled and professional workers who constitute a considerable 'brain drain' of skilled/mental labour (Jaafari, 1973). The number of Palestinian Arab refugees who are registered with UNRWA has grown from 960,021 in 1950 to 1,506,640 in 1972 (Hagopian and Zahlan, 1974). Additional pressure on the migration and flight of Palestinians has come from the use of Israel's five laws of land confiscation which are aimed at settling Jews in the territories, separating Arab villages from the fedayeen and encouraging Arab migration out of Israel and the territories (Jiryis, 1973; Jiryis, 1976; Ayyash, 1976).

Following Avineri's argument, it may be the case that the conversion of a backward Arab peasantry into a working class is an example of modernisation which has been brought about by the universalistic urges of Israeli capitalism, but it is certainly not an unambiguous, unidimensional process of development. The Arab labour force is part of Israel's industrial reserve army and the Arab worker is essentially a rural refugee who is forced to contribute surplus value via employment in occasional, seasonal occupations in agriculture, construction industries and petty commodity production. While the Israeli economy enjoys the benefits of a new market and cheap labour, the territories have been set upon a path of dependent and distorted development.

The only class to flourish under the conditions imposed by the Israeli authorities has been the merchant bourgeoisie (Hilal, 1976). The growth of the import-export trade between Israel and the territories, the growth of sub-contracting in Gaza for Israeli enterprises and the emergence of small businesses (citrus-packing houses) contributed to the survival of the traditional, merchant capitalist. By contrast, the starvation of Arab investment in industrial capital, competition from Israeli goods, and the favourable terms for Israeli capitalists (Ryan, 1974) have curtailed the development of an Arab industrial capitalist class. Both the agricultural and industrial wings of the Arab bourgeoisie lack confidence in the prospects for long-term investment. Finally, the traditional petty bourgeoisie (merchants, shopkeepers and artisans) has declined under the impact of Israeli capital and the loss of the tourist trade. The number of employers and semi-employed on the West Bank and Gaza declined from 43,000 in 1969 to 30,000 in 1973. The new petty bourgeoisie (teachers, technicians and professionals), while numerous, is forced to sell its mental labour on an international market outside Israel and the territories.

Neither Hegel's armchair Orientalism nor Avineri's equation of direct, intense colonisation with the maximum opportunities for modernisation provides an adequate theoretical analysis of the characteristic syndrome of underdevelopment and dependency which typifies the Arabs in Israel and the territories. The West Bank and Gaza Strip have had various opportunities for industrial capitalist development blocked by the special arrangements and privileges which protect and foster the Israeli economy at the expense of the Arab economy. While merchant capital flourishes as an agent of foreign capital, the Arab labour force exists as an unskilled, seasonal, migrant input into the Israeli economy to take up necessary positions in boom periods in the Israeli system. While all of these developments contradict the empirical claims which have been made by Avineri and others, the central failure of Avineri's theoretical system lies in his ideological reinterpretations of Marx's commentaries on Asian societies. Further criticism of Avineri will, therefore, involve an inspection of the theoretical validity of the concept of the AMP.

In contemporary Marxism, the AMP has been the object of considerable theoretical debate which has left the status, not only of the AMP, but of 'modes of production' as a scientific concept in doubt (Lichtheim, 1963; CERM, 1969; Anderson, 1974a, 1974b). The most comprehensive and damaging critique of the AMP and of the 'idealist epistemology' which underlies Avineri's use of the concept has been presented by Hindess and Hirst (1975). They reject any attempt to construct a theory of the AMP by random selection of quotations from Marx's journalism and letters without regard to their specific location in Marx's theoretical development. Since the journalism belongs to Marx's pre-scientific writings, the only theoretically proper site for a Marxist theory of the AMP will be in *Capital* and, to a lesser extent, in the *Grundrisse*. In other words, the theory of the AMP is to be found, not in Marx and Engels' overt commentary on colonialism and Asia, but in Marx's theoretical analyses of the general characteristics of 'modes of production' as objects of theoretical work. Avineri's interpretation of Marx rests, by contrast, almost solely on Marx's journalism, of which Marx himself made the comment that this 'continual newspaper muck annoys me . . . Purely scientific works are something completely different' (quoted in McLellan, 1973, p. 284). However, the real thrust of Hindess and Hirst's criticism is not whether Marx happened to think his journalism was 'muck', or whether the AMP happened to put in a conceptual appearance in *Capital*, but whether the AMP as a theoretical construct is coherent and logically determinate.

A mode of production is 'an articulated combination of a specific mode of appropriation of the product and specific mode of appropriation of nature' (Hindess and Hirst, 1975, p. 183). Relations of production define the form of surplus-labour appropriation and the distribution of the means of production (and therefore the relationship between labourers and non-labourers). Forces of production refer to the labour process by which raw material ('nature') is transformed into a product.

Thus, a mode of production is a complex unity of relations of production and forces of production in which relations of production are the dominant component of that unity. One feature of this definition is that it rejects the technological determinism which is typically involved in the notion that the forces determine the relations of production. The mode of appropriation of the surplus-product presupposes a distinct structure of relations of production which in turn supposes forces of production corresponding to the conditions of the labour process. In short, a theoretically adequate concept of 'mode of production' must be based on non-arbitrary articulations of forces/relations of production. The mode of appropriation of the surplus-product will provide a clue or theoretical indicator in the first instance for the presence or absence of a valid mode of production. The theoretical validity of the AMP is initially approached by considering what specific mode of appropriation corresponds to the AMP.

In pre-capitalist agriculture, the direct producers are not entirely separated from the means of production and the labourer retains part of the product. There is a low development of wage-labour and the local community is characterised by a unity of handicraft and agriculture. Because the producers are not wholly alienated from the means of production (the land), there is no simple *economic* mechanism for extracting a surplus. Pre-capitalist agriculture consequently requires extra-economic means to insure the appropriation of a surplus and this takes the form of political/ideological subordination of direct producers to non-producers. Various political/ideological structures intervene to support the appropriation of a surplus which takes the form of rent (labour-rent, rent in kind, money rent). These political and ideological structures are thus conditions of existence of that mode. In Asian societies, according to Marx, where the state 'stands over' direct producers as both landlord and sovereign, taxes and rents 'coincide, or rather, there exists no tax which differs from this form of ground-rent' and under these special conditions there is no requirement for 'stronger political and economic pressure than that common to all subjection to that state' (1970, Vol. 3, p. 791). This is the tax/rent couple resulting from the coupling of political sovereignty and land ownership in the state which appropriates surplus-product through taxation which is simultaneously a land-rent.

The question concerning the theoretical validity of the AMP now becomes more specific, namely, whether there is a mode of production which corresponds to the tax/rent couple? A variety of social relations are conditions of existence of the tax/rent couple. These include (1) a social division of labour between direct producers and non-labourers; (2) private property in land being absent, property rights are held by the state; (3) the state appropriates the surplus-product in the form of taxes which may be collected through a number of mechanisms (state officials or tax farmers); (4) there is political control of the distribution of the means of production by the state; (5) there is a unity of handicraft and agriculture; (6) there is no dominant class which is differentiated from the state bureaucracy; (7) consumption of the surplus-product is ideologically/politically determined and takes the form of either luxurious living by state officials or construction of public monuments by *corvée* labour; (8) the state may assume a variety of different forms (theocracy, tribal confederacy or colonial administration, for example). Hindess and Hirst argue on the basis of these social relations which are entailed by the tax/rent couple that it is theoretically impossible to establish an 'articulated combination of relations/forces of production' which corresponds to the tax/rent couple. This impossibility results from the fact that this mode of appropriation corresponds to two distinct forces of production, namely, independent peasant cultivation and communal cultivation. Both types of forces of production are compatible with the tax/rent couple. The production process and forces of production stand in an arbitrary relationship to the relations of production and so there can be no articulated combination of forces/relations of production. There is one additional feature of the AMP which rules it out as a scientific concept of a determinate mode of production. Independent peasant cultivation and communal cultivation do not in themselves presuppose the existence of social classes, but the tax/rent couple does suppose the existence of the state. However, the state does require the existence of social classes since it is only possible to explain the presence of the state on the basis of class struggle. The state exists to reproduce the general conditions of surplus appropriation in a social formation based on class antagonisms. Yet, there are no classes in the AMP because the state is the sole landlord and thus there is no dominant class independent of the state bureaucracy. The AMP is thus founded on a theoretical contradiction that the tax/rent couple presupposes the state but cannot explain the conditions of existence of the state in the absence of social classes. Hindess and Hirst conclude, therefore, that the AMP does not exist as a scientifically valid conception of an articulated combination of forces and relations of production.

Hindess and Hirst's formulations in *Pre-Capitalist Modes of Production* have been criticised on a number of grounds (Taylor, 1975 and 1976; Asad and Wolpe, 1976). In their more recent publications, Hindess and Hirst (1977) have themselves gone a long way to demolish the epistemological and conceptual foundations of their analysis of modes of production. Much of this critical debate has centred around the problems which are involved in formulating the relationships between social classes, modes of production and social formations. These problems constitute the main issues of Chapters 3, 4 and 5 in this study. At this stage I shall raise some initial difficulties in connection with Hindess and Hirst's original theoretical position before advancing to their self-criticisms in subsequent discussion of social classes and revolutions in the Middle East.

In *Pre-Capitalist Modes of Production*, Hindess and Hirst make a distinction between the abstract analysis of concepts and their relationships and the analysis of concrete social formations and conjunctures. While the study of concrete conjunctures is itself a work of theory, the analysis of concepts must precede a Marxist analysis of social formations. Following Poulantzas (1973, p. 15), they define a 'social formation' as a complex unity of social relations (economic, ideological and political structures) in which the economy is determinant. More directly, a social formation is a mode of production and its conditions of existence. Thus, a 'social formation' in Marxist analysis 'may loosely be said to correspond' to the sociological notion of a 'society' (Hindess and Hirst, 1975, p. 13). In Poulantzas' work we find the claim that the 'only thing which really exists' is a given social formation, that is, 'a social whole, in the widest sense, at a given moment in its historical existence: e.g. France under Louis Bonaparte, England during the Industrial Revolution' (Poulantzas, 1973, p. 15). There are five initial problems associated with the contrast between 'pure' modes of production and 'concrete' social formations. First, the distinction is based on precisely the empiricist epistemology which Poulantzas, Hindess and Hirst wish to reject. It reproduces the empiricist distinction in sociology between the theoretical analysis of 'social systems' and the empirical study of 'actual' societies (Asad and Wolpe, 1976, p. 471; Hindess and Hirst, 1977, ch. 1). Secondly, especially in the work of Poulantzas, the substitution of 'social formation' for 'society' is merely a terminological, not a conceptual substitution—it *is* simply a loose 'correspondence'. Thirdly, while these analytical works are supposed to be preliminary to the analysis of 'concrete conjunctures', this promise is only rarely and ambiguously fulfilled. The precise bearing of the theory of modes of production on the analysis of class struggles in concrete conjunctures remains ambiguous. In the absence of a clear account of the relationship between the theoretical and the concrete, the typical practice is simply to cite Lenin's *The Development of Capitalism in Russia* as an instance of adequate theoretical analysis in relation to a concrete conjuncture. Within this particular field, Marxism lacks an adequate 'methodology' of theoretical work which would clearly demonstrate how one proceeds from the 'raw material' of quasi-scientific concepts (Generalities I) to knowledge of the concrete (Generalities III) through the means for the production of knowledge (Generalities II) in the Althusserian epistemology (Althusser, 1969, ch. 6). Finally, when Poulantzas, or Hindess and Hirst, want to define a social formation in practice, they do this by ostensive definition, that is, by citing a particular nation-state (for example, France). In the pre-capitalist, pre-colonial Middle East such ostensive definitions of social formations become highly problematic. The use of such terms as

'Lebanon' or 'Algeria' are at best convenient and at worst highly misleading. To regard the imperial structure of the Ottoman system as an
appropriate object of concrete analysis would be to disregard its internal
diversity. Other distinctions—such as the Al Mashraq/Al Maghreb
dichotomy—are equally misleading, because they are formulated in
terms of commonsense categories.

It is a commonplace for Marxists to regard the social formations of the
underdeveloped world as constituted by a variety of overlapping modes
of production. As the CMP penetrates these social formations via
imperialism and colonialism, the complex pre-capitalist modes of a given
social formation are conserved and subordinated by the dominant CMP.
Thus, the Maghreb can be analysed as a social formation within which a
number of modes existed in a complex pattern before and after the
arrival of direct colonialism (Seddon, 1977). Assuming that one did
accept the theoretical adequacy of the AMP in studying the social formations of the Middle East, one would have to analyse its articulation with
other modes of production, pre-capitalist and capitalist, its subordination to the CMP via merchant capital and its dissolution (Keyder, 1976;
Islamoğlu and Keyder, 1977). Poulantzas specifically regards social
formations as complex combinations of overlapping modes of production and analyses the capitalist social formations of Europe in terms of
combinations of modes of production. Hindess and Hirst's conceptualisation of the mode and its conditions of existence, however, actually
rules out the possibility of such overlapping combinations. In *Pre-
Capitalist Modes of Production*, we are told that the structure of the
economic level of a social formation is governed by a variant of a given
mode of production 'but it may also include certain elements of other
modes' (Hindess and Hirst, 1975, p. 15) provided that these 'elements'
do not contradict the conditions of existence which are necessary for the
dominant mode. The implication of the argument is that different modes
of production cannot have the same conditions of existence. For
example, the transition of the dominance of FMP to CMP within a social
formation involves the non-reproduction of the conditions of existence
of the FMP. In their subsequent publications, Hindess and Hirst have
been quite explicit about this position, namely, their rejection of 'the
notion of social formation as a hierarchical combination of modes of
production' (1977, p. 47). The argument that a social formation is a
single, dominant mode of production and its conditions of existence
raises a number of difficult problems. It is difficult to explain the
presence of other 'elements' in a social formation since they cannot be
explained as effects of the reproduction of the dominant mode and they
must have their own conditions of existence. In their own analysis of the
transition from FMP to CMP, they appear in fact to demonstrate that
the absolutist state was a condition of existence of the FMP as the
dominant mode and also of 'capitalist' production. If the concept of

social formation is not defined in terms of overlapping modes of production, it is difficult to see how problems of contradictions and transitions in concrete conjunctures can be adequately theorised (Asad and Wolpe, 1976, pp. 501-5).

In principle it should be theoretically possible to generate an infinite range of abstract modes of production. Given the epistemological premises of *Pre-Capitalist Modes of Production*, there should be no definite limitations on the types of articulated combinations of relations and forces of production with their necessary conditions of existence. In addition, each of these possible modes of production would define a number of specific variant forms of the mode. For example, the FMP is a mode of production in which the surplus-labour is appropriated as rent, but this appropriation may take variant forms (rent in money, labour or kind). On the basis of my claim that there should in principle be no necessary limit to the number of modes of production which are possible, it is somewhat remarkable that Hindess and Hirst after all their analytical deliberations should end up with a list of modes which are generally acceptable among empiricist Marxists—primitive, slave, feudal and capitalist modes. Furthermore, their rejection of the AMP is not exactly an innovation; the Leningrad Conference of 1931 dismissed the AMP in terms of the analysis of most Asiatic societies. If we combine this limitation on the range of theoretically possible modes of production with Hindess and Hirst's rejection of the notion of overlapping modes of production within a social formation, it means that each social formation of the Middle East would have to be conceptualised in terms of the dominance of either PMP or SMP or FMP prior to the dominance of Western capitalism. In the light of their discussion of the tax/rent couple, one would assume (although it is by no means clear) that they would theorise the pre-capitalist formations of the Middle East in terms of the dominance of some variant form of the FMP. Unfortunately this option threatens to drive Hindess and Hirst toward a position of 'quasi-universal feudalism' (Anderson, 1974b, p. 484).

Hindess and Hirst base their argument on the claim that it is only in Marx's mature work, after the epistemological break of 1857 (Althusser, 1969, p. 35), that one can locate a scientific theory of modes of production. In practice, this criterion means that they focus almost exclusively on *Capital* to the neglect of works like the *Grundrisse* (1857/8) which must be included in the category of 'mature work'. What the *Grundrisse* provides is a range of pre-capitalist modes of production—Slav, Asiatic, classical, Germanic and nomadic—which provide 'avenues' out of primitive communalism. This range of modes has the merit of providing a basis for avoiding the sort of 'stagism' and unilinear views of history which are closely tied to the conventional Marxist emphasis on 'feudalism' as a privileged, global mode of production. It is precisely the difficulties associated with the application of the feudal mode outside

Europe which contribute to the perennial resurrections of the Asiatic mode as a conceptual framework (Rodinson, 1966; Melotti, 1977). One problem with Hindess and Hirst's treatment of these issues is that it is restricted to a rather narrow selection of pre-capitalist modes of production (Hobsbawm, 1964).

In this chapter I have concentrated on the use of the concept of the Asiatic mode as a basis for explaining the absence of capitalist development and political modernisation in Arabic societies. Avineri's attempt to provide a Marxist theory of Arab backwardness can be shown to be defective on both empirical and analytical grounds. This critique of Avineri is, however, somewhat incomplete since it illustrates quite clearly many of the unresolved theoretical problems which surround the contemporary debate in Marxism about the correct analysis of modes of production and their laws of motion. There are, of course, many excellent Marxist accounts of Middle East social formations (Farsoun, 1975), but these primarily descriptive surveys leave the major theoretical difficulties unresolved. Having examined certain basic issues in Marxist approaches to the Middle East, it is now possible to contrast the dominant Orientalist model of Islamic society as a mosaic of social groups with various Marxist perspectives.

3

Ethnicity, Social Class and the Mosaic Model

The classical Orientalist tradition did not concern itself overmuch with problems of social structure, still less with issues of political economy. In so far as Orientalists had an image or 'theory' of a social structure which they termed 'Islamic', they described the Islamic social system as a set of autonomous, separate, vertical units. In *Islamic Society and the West*, Gibb and Bowen (1950, Vol. 1, p. 159) provide a clear statement of the view of modern Orientalists that under Islam the 'ruled' were split up into many semi-independent units (such as tribes, trade guilds, villages and communities) whose social 'stability was little affected by the political vicissitudes of the Empire as a whole'. Islamic society did not take the form of an integrated social unity but rather was constituted by a mosaic of isolated, self-supporting 'social groups'. This particular view of the mosaic is also closely associated with the traditional idea that social stratification in Islam was primarily along religious lines (Shiloh, 1969). For example, it is often pointed out that as Islam conquered the Middle East and North Africa it accorded a degree of legitimacy, continuity and self-government to Christians who were regarded as 'People of the Book'. This tradition was evolved under the Ottoman Empire into an institutionalised *millet* system whereby a high degree of autonomy and internal self-government was given to various religious minorities, such as Christians, Jews and Armenians (Lewis, 1961). At the beginning of this century, the Turkish government recognised fourteen autonomous *millets* (Hourani, 1947). In addition to taking cognizance of these vertical pillars or *millets*, the conventional literature on the Middle East burgeons with constant references to the diverse ethnic composition of the 'Islamic peoples'. For many anthropologists, the 'most conspicuous fact' about Middle East society is that 'in each country the population consists of a mosaic of peoples' (Coon, 1951, p. 2).

Islamic social structure is conceived, then, as a mosaic or patchwork of tribes, religious minorities, social groups and associations. This massive diversity is furthermore treated as a major weakness of Islamic society and as a flaw within the social structure. Because of the internal diversity of the social system, it was necessarily difficult to organise consistent, coherent opposition to the authoritarian rule of the imperial household. The theory of the mosaic society is, therefore, an adjunct of the theory of Oriental Despotism. The mosaic diversity of the social structure provides a 'natural' context for an arbitrary ruler who can divide and rule without fear of integrated and co-ordinated opposition. While the ruler enjoys absolute power, each village, community and location is divided into warring social factions (Gibb and Bowen, 1950, p. 268). The Orientalist view of fractionalism in the Islamic social structure is nowhere better illustrated than in the descriptions of city life which are the commonplace assumptions of Orientalist urban geography. The Middle East city was sharply divided into urban quarters which were social, geographical and administrative units (Lapidus, 1969a). These separate quarters also had strong ethnic and religious features which distinguished them as social communities within the urban framework. According to the Orientalist conception, while these quarters had a certain intra-social solidarity, there was little inter-societal integration because there were few socio-cultural connections between the urban quarters. City life consequently was riven by factionalism and political life was primarily a matter of alliances between various urban and rural elites who attempted to manipulate the mass through a system of criminal gangs. The final component of the Orientalist view of despotism and fissiparous city life is supplied by Ibn Khaldun's theory of elite circulation between rural bedouin and their urban counterpart. While the cities are centres of religious and commercial life, they lack certain crucial aspects of urban and social integration. This weakness of the Islamic city allows bedouin tribesmen who possess great 'group feeling' (*asabiyya*) to displace the urban elites periodically from their position of social dominance. The dynamic elements within the social mosaic are the gyrations of powerful elites whose political movements leave the patchwork structure still intact.

The mosaic theory (Oriental Despotism, the divided city and circulating elites) produces one important theoretical difficulty. Given the centrality of factionalism, the threat of mob rule, and the absence of social ties at the macro-societal level, it is difficult to see how the mosaic theory could prevent Islamic society from dissolving into a ceaseless internal war of anarchy and conflict. Orientalists have solved 'the Hobbesian problem of order' by claiming that Islam provides a system of central values and beliefs which was capable of uniting and integrating the social system through such institutional mechanisms as the Sufi brotherhoods, the '*ulama* and the *Shar'ia*. This solution, however, invites us to regard Islam as a timeless, monolithic and homogeneous culture which provides a perfectly adequate device for syphoning off the internal, factional conflicts of the social structure. The mosaic model of 'Islamic society' is not, therefore, especially convincing since it requires us to believe that this social system was both completely integrated around Islamic values and totally divided in terms of ethnicity, stratification and association. The mosaic model also requires an acceptance of the assumption that this patchwork society experienced occasional revolts but never underwent any real revolutionary restructuring of the social system.

This particular view of Islamic social organisation is not restricted to Orientalist historians but is also widely reproduced in the contemporary research of sociologists and political scientists. For example, Bill (1972) rejects any analysis of the stratification system of the Middle East which is based exclusively on Marxist concepts of economic classes because other forms of power have generally been more significant in the area. Thus, 'political influence, personal manipulation, saintly ancestry and traditional education generally superseded wealth' (Bill, 1972, p. 420) in shaping the social structure with the result that 'modes of maneuver' have been more significant than modes of production. While Bill attempts to modify and extend the Marxian analysis of economic classes through Weberian categories of status and power which he derives from Ralf Dahrendorf, Gerhard Lenski and Talcott Parsons, in fact he merely reproduces the old mosaic model of Oriental Despotism. For example, the stratification system is treated as a complex system of overlapping social groups in 'a system-preserving balance of tension' (Bill, 1972, p. 430) in which power relations are constituted by the intrigues between circulating elites. The key feature of political life is, in Weberian terms, the arbitrary and rapid promotion or social mobility of individuals who have 'learned to maneuver and utilize the less obvious facets of power' (Bill, 1972, p. 432). Political life generally is characterised by fissiparous conflicts. However, this mass of 'intraclass divisions and tensions' has paradoxically contributed to the stability of the whole system, the basic structure of which has 'weathered the change of dynasty, elite, monarch and invader' (Bill, 1972, p. 432). Although the system has been modified by the rise of a new middle class of professionals and technicians with the modernisation of Turkey, Egypt and Tunisia, this class has been unable to change the system at its root because it is 'hampered' by intra-class conflicts and divisions.

In this particular example we can detect the reproduction of the conventional assumptions of the Orientalist tradition—political intrigue, historical stagnation, mosaic stratification—despite the importation of a new sociological terminology. Attempts such as Bill's to replace Marxism by a sociology of stratification can be criticised on a number of different grounds. Bill mistakenly assumes that Marx's class analysis is an attempt to describe the empirical inequalities of wealth between individuals or social groups within a society. But economic classes cannot be reduced to inequalities between individuals or defined in terms of cut-off points in a multidimensional cluster of hierarchies of power, status and wealth, because economic classes do not refer to relations of distribution in a market but to the relations of production. Ultimately Bill reduces the class structure to the capacities of individuals (their ability to learn the techniques of manoeuvre and intrigue) or to a descriptive list of the social groups which appear to be present in a social system without an explanation of the constitution of these groups through the political, ideological and economic structures of the mode of production. This social psychology of group relationships is encased within the archaic assumptions of Oriental Despotism, in which the mosaic is cemented together by a near-magical 'system-preserving balance of tension'.

Unfortunately, this perspective on the balanced mosaic which perpetually reproduces its own historical stagnation is not restricted to functionalist theories in sociology. For example, it is possible to construct a mosaic theory of the Middle East from Marx's view in the *Grundrisse* that the fragmented, self-sufficient village communities provide a solid foundation for 'Asiatic despotism'. Thus, Abrahamian (1974, 1975) employs a Marxist version of the mosaic model to provide an account of the social organisation of Qajar Iran. In this view, whereas the estates of feudal Europe were 'viable collectives', the social orders (*tabaqat*) of Iran 'were sharply divided into small vertical communities ... and the general population, both urban and rural, was fragmented into conflicting groups—into warring tribes, villages and even town wards' (Abrahamian, 1975, p. 138). This complex and diversified social structure 'prevented latent socio-economic classes from developing into active political forces' (Abrahamian, 1975, p. 148). This mosaic theory of Iran which is partly drawn from Marx's *Grundrisse* is, therefore, another avenue towards the familiar AMP thesis that there were no classes within the Asiatic structure. The notion that the Islamic Middle East is a patchwork of social groups leads eventually to the Hegelian conclusion that it is a society without a 'civil society', that is, a form of social organisation without a network of interlocking and interconnecting social linkages and associations (Mardin, 1969).

Orientalists' conceptions of the social structure of the Middle East have been stimulated by the problem of imposing despotic order in a context of diversity, if not anarchy. In the Ottoman system, the autonomous vertical units of *millets*, tribes and villages were held together by the cultural roofing provided by Islam. Orientalist studies of North Africa, especially in the case of Morocco which was not occupied by the Ottoman Turks, present an interesting variation on the dominant mosaic theme. The patchwork of the Maghreb is seen to be constituted by a fundamental ethnic division between Berber and Arab. Typically, Berbers have been regarded by the early French administrators/anthropologists as 'Noble Savages' living in a state of tribal democracy in opposition to the 'Ignoble Arab' whose political tradition is one of despotism. This 'Kabyle myth' was first generated in the early days of French colonial intervention in Algeria and found its most cogent expression in Hanoteau and Letourneux's *La Kabylie et les coutumes Kabyles* (1893). The original myth of Berber democracy versus Arab despotism was further elaborated in the context of French control over Morocco. The dominant anthropological image of the political system was a split polity containing dissident Berbers (*Bled es-Siba*) and a central Arab, tax-collecting government (*Bled el-Makhzan*). The political system was constituted 'by contradictory tendencies toward autocratic order and anarchy, in which neither [dissident Berbers nor government] was able to gain the upper hand' (Burke, 1973, p. 175). The political split was also religious and legal in nature. The berbers held to their customary laws and local saints in opposition to the holy law and orthodox *'ulama* of the towns (Gellner, 1969). Once more the dynamic aspect of the model is provided by Ibn Khaldun's theory of elite circulation. The dissident tribes depend upon the towns for certain goods (firearms, grain, cloth) and the city merchants depend on rural tribesmen as clients for basic and luxury goods (Burke, 1969), but the town dwellers also live in fear of the threat of tribal raids on the town and its supply routes. While the 'Berber myth' and tribal circulation theory suggest that the tribes exist in a condition bordering on constant anarchy, the conventional anthropology of Morocco also requires the notion that the tribes are very tightly integrated and enjoy considerable social solidarity (*asabiyya*). By contrast, the town is defined in the Orientalist tradition by three absences—an independent civic administration, an autonomous bourgeoisie and social solidarity (Al-Azmeh, 1976). The political history of the towns of North Africa is thus treated as a matter of tribal circulations whereby the social vacuum of the town is periodically dispersed by the 'group feeling' of incoming tribesmen (Gellner, 1972).

The mosaic theory of the Middle East social structure attempts to draw attention to supposed differences between the social organisation and history of European societies and the Islamic world. The central assumption is that while European societies from feudalism to capitalism can be adequately conceptualised in terms of a system of social stratification whose primary units are those of social class, the social structure of Islam can only be described in terms of semi-autonomous vertical units. Within this mosaic of units, economic class is relatively unimportant when compared to ethnicity, religion and tribe. Furthermore, the Marxist version of the concept of 'social class' is usually held to be too vulgar or too ideological to be of service in the analysis of Middle East societies. The modes of production—slavery, feudalism and capitalism—in the conventional Marxist scheme are regarded by most Orientalists as systems of 'class-dominated' politics, and these schemes can only be applied to the Middle East when they have been radically redefined (Zartman, 1976). In so far as Orientalists in the social sciences are prepared to accept an analysis of the area in terms of some notion of 'social stratification', they typically employ a multidimensional and pluralist view of stratification (van Nieuwenhuijze, 1965). This pluralist view, as we shall discover, is basically a sociological version of the traditional mosaic model in which the concept of 'social strata' is merely grafted on to the list of existing 'social groups' of ethnicity and religion. The *locus classicus* of the sociological critique of Marxist theories of economic classes and modes of production is to be found in the work of Max Weber. In particular, Weber's view of Islamic society comes very near to being a comprehensive summation and condensation of all the streams of analysis—history, economics, religious studies, sociology—which constitute the Orientalist conception of the Middle East.

There is no need here to rehearse the full gamut of Max Weber's criticisms of Marx's sociology. Weber *claimed* to differ from Marx on at least three important issues. First, he argued that causal explanations without meaningful interpretation of interpersonal, social actions were inadequate. The causal analysis of capitalist relations of production presupposes an adequate understanding of 'capitalist actions' at the level of human meaning (Outhwaite, 1975). Secondly, he argued that the superstructure of political, legal and religious beliefs and institutions cannot be 'read off' directly and simply from the economic base. Weber approached the social system, therefore, as a complex unity of independent institutional orders—economy, polity, law, religion—which interact with each other in ways which cannot be readily comprehended in terms of general, law-like statements. Thirdly, given the relative autonomy of the institutional fabric of society, the emphasis given to 'economic factors' in the definition of social stratification is too narrow. Weber consequently modified Marx's view that social classes are defined by relations of production by treating social classes as groups in relation to social distribution (the market). Social classes are constituted by persons in the same class situation in relation to a market where skills can be sold for a wage. In addition, Weber recognised 'honour' and 'power' as crucial features of social stratification which cannot be reduced to economic conditions (Giddens, 1973). While social classes are not collectivities, they may provide under special conditions the social basis for collective action. By contrast, status groups are definite social communities, bound together by a common culture and similar social interests. Similarly, differences in the social distribution of power find their institutionalised expression through the vehicle of political parties. The effect of these conceptual distinctions in the eyes of most sociologists is to produce a more flexible and more subtle analysis of social stratification as a multidimensional system of economic, political and social inequality.

Whether or not these three issues in fact distinguish Weber's sociology from that of Marx is a matter of unsettled controversy. In part, Weber's critique amounts to an attack on Marxism as it was presented by intellectuals associated with the Social Democratic Party toward the end of the nineteenth century rather than a significant objection to Marx as such (Giddens, 1972). There are, as I hope to show in this and the following two chapters, a variety of cogent replies to Weberian criticisms of historical materialism. However, if we distinguish between what Weber claimed to do in sociology (such as his statements about epistemology and methodology) and what he actually achieved (in his sociology of civilisations), then there are some remarkable areas of overlap between Weber and Marx. For example, there are close connections between Weber's Orientalism and Marx's Hegelianism and this is especially obvious in the parallels between Weber's concept of 'patrimonialism' and Marx's analysis of Asiatic society. This proximity of perceptions, of course, gives additional urgency to attempts by writers like Hindess and Hirst to demonstrate the ideological underpinnings of the theoretically inadequate AMP.

Weber's Orientalism emerges out of his attempt to explain the rise of European capitalism in the context of a variety of cross-cultural comparisons. In order to make those comparisons Weber employs a basic dichotomy between the feudal economies of the West and the prebendal/patrimonial political economies of the East. In Weber's sociology, feudalism is a system where, in return for military service, a military stratum enjoys certain privileges which can be inherited by virtue of a stable set of legal norms. The prebend, by contrast to the feu, is a specific set of privileges which cannot be transmitted routinely from one generation of military families to the next generation. The fundamental difference between the two systems is not really a question of differences in land-rents but a political difference between land-owning warlords and the central authority (the state). Feudal landlords are relatively autonomous *vis-à-vis* the centre (whether monarchy or state) but closely linked to the local peasantry and region. Under prebendalism, the centre is strong and landlords are simply office-holders under contract without specific, parochial links to peasantry and region (Wallerstein, 1974). Patrimonial empires based on prebendal contracts tend to experience severe fiscal crises because of problems in the money supply for state officials and the imperial bureaucracy. If the empire expands through conquest, there is usually sufficient booty to pay off imperial armies and the state officialdom. Failure to expand means that loyalty to the centre can only be bought by changing the nature of the prebendal contract. This fiscal crisis tends to find its solution either in a 'feudalisation' of the prebend or in tax-farming arrangements or both. These developments within the Islamic states were, for Weber, major causes of the failure of commercialisation and capitalist development (Weber, 1968, p. 1016).

Weber's analysis of prebendalism is parallel to Marx's account of the tax/rent couple in *Capital,* and both approaches provide a preliminary outline of social formations and modes of production which could avoid the Hegelianised versions of the AMP which have been considered in previous chapters. Unfortunately, Weber overlays this discussion of Islamic prebendalism with two additional components which have become the staples of the internalist version of development—the 'Islamic ethic' and the absence of an entrepreneurial urban bourgeoisie. Weber's argument that Islam made no dynamic, ascetic claims on personality, and positively encouraged acceptance of 'this world', is unconvincing (Turner, 1974b). His other observations on the ways in which the Holy Law prevented commercial development, rationalisation of commerce and usurious capital are equally false (Rodinson, 1966). The inadequacies of Weber's views on Islamic culture have not, however, prevented later scholars from attempting to discover analogies of the Protestant Ethic in various Muslim communities (Bellah, 1963). Sociologists have also been dominated by what one might term Weber's 'problematic of the missing middle class'. Because of the peculiarities of a sacred law which cannot change rationally to meet new contingencies and because of the interference from patrimonial despots, the landlords, merchants and state officials do not enjoy security of person and property. These strata, therefore, invest their wealth in *waqf* property which, because it is formally committed to some religious purpose, is relatively safe from despotic sequestration. Wealth was consequently 'frozen' and did not lead to capital accumulation. Further limitations were set upon the development of a potential bourgeoisie by the fact that Islam, according to Weber, accorded social honour to servants of the state (soldiers and officials) rather than to merchants so that imperial trade fell into the hands of minority groups, especially Christians and Jews (Sussnitzki, 1966). The mosaic structure of the Islamic city and the militaristic ethos of Islam inhibited the development of a creative middle class of industrialists and merchants. While an autonomous, urban bourgeoisie was 'missing', the most prominent 'fact' about the class structure of the Islamic city, according to most Orientalists, was that city life was dominated by prebendal landowners 'whose incomes derives from agriculture' (Baer, 1964, p. 207).

The task which appears to face writers on the Middle East stratification system in the modern world is to describe the similarities and differences between the European middle class whose 'birth constitutes the shift from estate society to class society' (van Nieuwenhuijze, 1965, p. 12) and the Islamic middle class whose absence partly explains the absence of capitalist democracy in the Middle East. The focal issues of these studies are the role of the state in the process of Middle East industrialisation and the emergence of a new middle class of technicians, civil servants and army officers. We can take the case of the Egyptian class structure as an example of these issues. The Egyptian working class engaged in industrial production represents a small fraction of the total labour force. According to the 1947 census, the working class (factory, construction, transport workers and others) amounted to approximately

400,000 workers in an employed population of 6.5 million. The great majority of workers are concentrated in unskilled and semi-skilled occupations in agriculture. Within the working population, therefore, the industrial proletariat accounts for about 6 per cent, artisans for 10 per cent, agricultural workers for 22 per cent and a mixed category of service workers ('the commercial office proletariat') for 11 per cent (Gordon and Fridman, 1964). By the beginning of the 1960s, the industrial working class had increased to around 550,000, while the white collar category of (mainly) government employees had risen from 1.2 million in 1947 to 1.5 million in 1960. The industrial capitalist class has, correspondingly, remained relatively small and insignificant, while the traditional petty bourgeoisie has declined in the face of competition from foreign goods and with the concentration of industrial production following Nasser's attempts to reorganise certain branches of industry. The main growth point of the Egyptian occupational structure has been the emergence of a new middle class (professionals, civil servants, teachers and scientific workers). This growth is partly accounted for by the extension of the public sector. For example, the number of government posts increased by around 61 per cent between 1940 and 1955 (Berger, 1957). However, the growth of the professional sector can be traced back to an earlier period. Between 1937 and 1947, the number of doctors and dentists increased from 3,700 to 6,300, while the number of engineers rose from 8,400 to 15,800 (Makarius, 1960). A brief summary of these figures points to the fact that in the economically active population of Egypt between 1958 and 1968 over 56 per cent of the population was engaged in agriculture, 17 per cent in services and only 10 per cent in industry (Berger, 1964; Baer, 1964; van Nieuwenhuijze, 1971).

These developments within the occupational structure of Egypt have suggested to a number of writers that Egypt is developing without the benefit of 'an independent middle class based upon manufacturing and commercial interests' (Berger, 1964) which was crucial to economic and political change in the West. Instead, the Egyptian middle class is constituted by government employees (technicians, teachers and soldiers) who are not independent and who have somewhat narrow interests in the continuity of specific governmental regimes. While an independent middle class of industrialists may be absent, it has been claimed that, especially in Egypt, the army is an instrument of the new middle class of salaried employees and that the army can exercise an independent, modernising role in underdeveloped societies (Halpern, 1962). Throughout the Middle East, according to this thesis, the growth of the state apparatus, in particular the military bureaucracy, provides a channel through which the new middle class can exercise political power. The new middle class's dominance within the military hierarchy provides a significant opportunity for national independence and social reform (Khadduri, 1955; Rustow, 1959; Janowitz, 1964).

The Halpern thesis concerning the integrative, modernising role of the Egyptian army as an instrument of the new middle class can be challenged on empirical grounds, namely, that the Egyptian army in politics has not brought about social stability and political democratisation (Perlmutter, 1967; Halpern, 1969; Perlmutter, 1970). The whole tradition in social science of treating the military as an organised, efficient elite capable of modernising the economy and social structure is based on dubious assumptions which have strong ideological implications (Vickery, 1972). Orientalists' accounts of social structure are riddled with confusion and misconception. A variety of terms—'bourgeoisie', 'merchant class' and 'middle class'—are all used interchangeably to describe a great diversity of intermediate strata. In reply to aspects of the Weber-Tawney debate, Orientalists have been at pains to show that Islam was not hostile to commercialism and to merchants and that consequently Islam was not an obstacle to capitalist development. The presence or absence of merchants and trade is, however, irrelevant as a condition for the transformation of the FMP. Merchants do not necessarily, so to speak, grow up into industrial capitalists. Merchant capital 'cannot by itself contribute to the overthrow of the old mode of production [FMP] but tends rather to preserve and retain it as its precondition' (Marx, 1970, Vol. 3, p. 334). Attempts by Orientalists to show that merchants (whom they wrongly describe as 'bourgeoisie') existed in medieval Islam and that consequently Islam was not incompatible with capitalism are founded on wholly inadequate assumptions (Goitein, 1957). The problematic of 'the missing middle class' falls into the typical internalist fallacy of assuming that the exact conditions of capitalist development in Britain in the seventeenth and eighteenth centuries could be nicely reproduced in the rest of the world in the nineteenth and twentieth centuries. Certainly Germany and Italy did not enjoy the 'benefits' of an independent, progressive middle class. The whole debate about entrepreneurship as a condition for capitalist development is either false or tautological (Baran, 1973, p. 385).

While these criticisms of the Halpern thesis are perfectly valid, they attack the doctrine of modernising elites at the wrong level. What is required primarily is an attack on the basic assumptions of the mosaic model. Whereas Orientalists treated 'classical Islam' as a mosaic of ethnic and religious collectivities in which politics involved circulating alliances between elites within the broad framework of Oriental Despotism, contemporary political scientists regard the Middle East as a patchwork of social groups and social classes in which politics involves elite struggles within the context of authoritarian government. The old mosaic was held together by Islam; the new mosaic is cemented together by the state equipped with nationalist ideology. What both variants of the mosaic model have in common is the belief that traditional Middle East societies were not 'class dominated' and that in the modern Middle

East 'social class' is only in the process of emerging alongside other forms of social stratification. The mosaic thesis, as a result, must deny the validity of large sections of Marxist theory in relation to the analysis of Middle East social formations. Anyone who wants to develop a Marxist analysis of North Africa and the Middle East must start with a critique of the mosaic theory and all its related assumptions.

It is not, of course, just a question of confronting an Orientalist rejection of the relevance of Marxist concepts for the study of the Middle East. A number of authors who work within a framework of Marxist assumptions have questioned the specific relevance of Marx's concepts of class and mode of production for the analysis of non-European social formations. In particular, a variety of commentators have argued that the concepts of 'feudalism' and 'feudal classes' have a restricted relevance in the context of a pre-capitalist Middle East (Duvignaud, 1963; Duvignaud, 1965; Avineri, 1968a; Smith, 1975). A forceful case against the use of conventional Marxist categories has been presented by Ahmad El Kodsy (Kodsy and Lobel, 1970) in his essay on 'Nationalism and Class Struggles in the Arab World'. El Kodsy divides the 'Arab World' into three sectors (Al Maghreb, Al Mashraq and the countries of the Nile) and argues that this world was not primarily rural and feudal, but urban and mercantile. Egypt, as a 'peasant civilization' extracting a surplus from 'cultivators of the soil', was the main exception. For the rest of the Arab world, partly because of the aridity of the climate and the backwardness of agricultural techniques, the surplus which could be extracted from peasant cultivators was very small and could not support a feudal class. Hence, 'the forms of social organization of this community are inevitably characterised by primitive collectivism' (Kodsy and Lobel, 1970, p. 5) but this appears to be the subordinate 'form of social organization'. The urban civilisations and their dominant classes were erected on the profits extracted from the trade between Asia and Europe. The Arab ruling class depended on 'an income derived, in the last analysis, from the surplus extracted by the ruling classes of other civilisations (the ones linked together by the Arab world) from their own peasantries' (Kodsy and Lobel, 1970, p. 6).

While some features of El Kodsy's thesis can be salvaged, the thesis as it stands contains at least two serious difficulties. Since El Kodsy is forced to argue that the forces of production condition the relations of production, his thesis involves either technological determinism or geographical/climactic determinism. Of course, Marx and Engels were themselves guilty of reducing the relations of production to geographical factors in their early formulations of the AMP. For example, in a letter to Marx in 1853, Engels claimed that the absence of private property in land 'even in its feudal form' was 'mainly due to the climate, taken in connection with the nature of the soil' (Marx and Engels, 1972, p. 314). The belief that class relations are determined in the last instance by the weather is not exactly convincing. The second difficulty in El Kodsy's position is the notion that the size of the rural surplus (or potential rural surplus) determines the presence of the FMP. In order for the FMP to be secured, there must be certain ideological/political conditions which allow a class of landlords to appropriate surplus-labour in the form of feudal rent where peasants have a degree of possession of the land. Feudal rent can take the form of rent in kind, in money, or in labour. Furthermore, there are problems involved in the equation of pastoral nomadism with the primitive communist mode of production. Also, the existence of intercontinental trade does not allow us to specify a distinct mode of production.

The great achievement of Hindess and Hirst in *Pre-Capitalist Modes of Production* (1975) was to have converted quasi-scientific concepts of 'feudalism' as a system of interpersonal obligations into a scientific concept of the structures of the FMP. The problem with Middle East studies is that we have hardly begun the work of assembling our quasi-scientific concepts in order to achieve such a massive transformation. The construction of concepts of modes of production is crucial since, as I shall elaborate in Chapter 5, it is impossible to formulate an adequate theory of social classes until we have a coherent view of the modes of production which are present in a given social formation. As a starting point, however, it would be possible to provide a list of the under-developed, quasi-scientific notions of social organisation which we do possess as a basis for developing more rigorous concepts of modes of production. The main protagonists for a place in the list of quasi-scientific conceptions for an analysis of Middle East social formations prior to the intervention of colonial capitalism are pastoral nomadism, prebendalism and feudalism. In addition, it will be important to provide some theoretical elaboration of the crucial role played by merchant capital and petty commodity production within the context of pre-colonial Middle East development.

The use of the term 'prebendalism' has at least one clear advantage over the concept of AMP (and related terms such as 'Oriental Despotism') in that prebendalism does not carry with it any geographical designation. By prebendalism I mean a system in which land is allocated to state officials, not as heritable property, but as a right to extract tribute from the peasantry (Wolf, 1966). In the Ottoman Empire, these landlords (*sipahis*) had a right to collect the traditional tax within a designated area (*timar*). The *sipahis* collected this rent in kind from independent peasant producers who were forced to carry this rent in kind to the nearest market. This system was gradually replaced after the sixteenth century by tax-farming methods. The state also extracted revenue by control of trade through custom duties and through the sale of concessions to merchants. The state controlled manufactures through the system of urban guilds, and supervised trade through its administrative control of the market place. So long as the state was able to retain control of trade, mercantile accumulation did not present a serious threat to prebendal forms of social organisation (Inalcik, 1969). The eventual dissolution of the traditional prebendal system was partly an effect of the state's loss of control over merchants with the growth of contraband trade following the demand for raw materials from the expanding European economy (Keyder, 1976). The rise in illegal trade in the hands of the great merchants resulted in a loss of state revenue, a decline in the trading cities of Bursa and Aleppo (Inalcik, 1960) and a commercialisation of agricultural production. As the central state was weakened through a significant loss of revenue, landlords at the periphery of the system came to enjoy a relative autonomy, and thus the rise of these independent lords (*ayans*) indicates a 'feudalisation' of the traditional prebendal organisation. These estates were rapidly integrated into the world economy by responding to the European demand for grain, tobacco and cotton. In order to satisfy this demand, independent peasant producers were brought under new exploitative relations of feudal serfdom or under various forms of share-cropping. Commercialised production for a market had the effect of intensifying exploitation with archaic forms of labour organisation since the peasantry was liable to the traditional taxes and to new forms of taxation introduced by the new class of feudal landlords. This integration of prebendal Ottoman structu: ̣s into the world market was, therefore, accompanied by a feudalisation of labour organisation (Islamoğlu and Keyder, 1977).

While the notions of prebendalism and feudalism in combination with forms of merchant capital and petty commodity production would provide some starting points for the analysis of social formations under the political control of the Ottoman Empire, it would be important to add some discussion of pastoral nomadism in the description of social formations in North Africa, Saudi Arabia and Iran. Whereas certain Soviet authors prefer to treat pastoral nomadism as a form of feudalism with patriarchal survivals, Perry Anderson (1974a, p. 220) points out that, from a reading of the *Grundrisse*, there are good grounds for treating nomadic pastoralism as a distinct mode of production. Transhumant pastoralism is typically based on individual ownership of the animal stock with collective access to pasture. It does not require ownership of land as property but merely rights of movement and access to water and pasture on a seasonal migratory basis. There is usually a complex relationship between settled and nomadic populations. Town dwellers often invest in herds which are then entrusted to nomads, while wealthy nomadic families invest in urban property. Nomads rarely practise cultivation except for seasonal barley (Abou-Zeid, 1968). This close interaction between settled and nomadic societies is the dominant characteristic of the semi-nomadism of the Middle East (Patai, 1951). The individual failure of nomads may result in sedentarisation and proletarianisation if these nomads are forced into the ranks of the unemployed in the *bidonvilles* of the Maghreb. The continuity of nomadic status is closely connected with the complex patterns of patronage which exist between and within tribes. Small client tribes are social buffers between large tribes while within tribes individual families are ranked in terms of their relationship to the nomadic nobility (Peters, 1968). The nomadic pastoralism of the Middle East also traditionally involved extensive forms of domestic slavery. These characteristics of transhumant pastoralism serve to differentiate this mode from feudalism and prebendalism; in addition, pastoralism cannot be easily classified as a form of primitive communism. There is private ownership of herds (despite the practice of common grazing) and failure to maintain this private property resulted in either sedentarisation or personal bondage.

These forms of undigested, quasi-scientific 'knowledge' could be the basis for generating a range of concepts of modes of production. For each mode of production, we would expect to identify a dominant and subordinate class with a range of intermediate classes, such as merchants. If after extensive conceptualisation it proved possible to characterise the social formations of the Middle East in terms of three modes of production prior to capitalist dependency—feudal, prebendal and nomadic—then we would expect the class system to be organised in terms of six basic classes at the level of theory. In concrete terms, the dominant classes would include nomadic sheikhs, feudal landlords and prebendal lords along with a merchant class, while the subordinate classes would be independent peasants, serfs or quasi-slaves. Such an approach would in principle allow us to conceptualise intra-class conflicts within the dominant power bloc, crises within pre-capitalist modes of production and transformations of modes. In short, this approach to the Middle East would avoid the ideological and theoretical difficulties of the conventional AMP which assumed no real history, no internal contradictions and no classes. An adequate characterisation of modes of production would also counter the argument that Marx's analysis of social formations requires an oversimplified view of a two-class model of class structure. The mosaic model would consequently be replaced by a theory of class based on an analysis of modes of production.

Unfortunately the generation of such an elaborate theory of classes and modes remains an unrealised project for future analytical work. While significant advances have been made in the analysis of social classes in monopoly capitalism and in the critique of Weberian theories of status groups (Poulantzas, 1975a), the analysis of pre-capitalist modes of production, the class structure of underdeveloped societies, and the role of ideological categories of ethnicity and religion remains to be accomplished. These problems confront Marxist theory at a variety of levels. At the theoretical and political level, the proper understanding of the superstructure and the notion of 'nation above class' are critically significant for a Marxism of the Middle East.

4

Ideology: Nationalism and the Superstructure

One of the primary objects of Orientalism is to establish a clear demarcation between the essence of European culture and history and the essence of Islamic Middle Eastern societies. The mosaic model thus serves to pinpoint fundamental differences between occidental feudalism based on estates or social classes and Oriental Despotism based on *millets* and ethnic diversity. Whereas feudalism contained within its structures the seeds of capitalism, Oriental Despotism merely reproduced its own stagnation. The mosaic of traditional Islam has, however, been shattered by the combined forces of Western colonialism, industrialisation and nationalism. From the Orientalist perspective, it is still important to emphasise the difference between the Western route to modern, industrial democracy and the Islamic path to the modern world. Since the routes were different, Orientalists argue that even when certain Islamic countries come close to achieving industrial modernisation, modernity in the Middle East is parasitic upon the Western model of secular democracy. The institutions of industrial capitalism in the Middle East are regarded as mimetic derivations from a pure Western stock. This cluster of attitudes is most pronounced in the case of Orientalist approaches to Arab nationalism. The usual position is either to condemn nationalism outright as an irrational intrusion into political life or to regard Arab nationalism as fraudulent and unnecessary.

The common feature of Orientalist approaches to nationalism in history, sociology and Islamics (Hodgson, 1974, Vol. 1, p. 56) is to cast the Middle East within an insoluble dilemma. Middle East political leaders covertly want to achieve Western standards of living with Western institutions and technology, but because of the history of colonialism and the strength of anticolonial attitudes it is impossible to have any overt commitment to Western culture and technology. In addition, Western values represent an affront to Islam and Islamic history. In Europe a certain degree of secularisation was a condition of national industrial development, but in the Middle East sanctity and puritanism (Gellner, 1963) are constitutive of anticolonial nationalism. In the view of Orientalism this situation leads to the paradox that Middle

East leaders are typically liberal and pro-Western in private, but have to be rigidly pious and anti-Western in public. In sociology, one influential source of the Orientalist viewpoint was provided by Daniel Lerner (1958) who suggested that a major hurdle in the way of successful modernisation was extreme nationalism and xenophobia. The dilemmas of adopting Westernisation and an anticolonial ideology are, in Lerner's view, nowhere better illustrated than in the case of Nasser's Egypt. The failure of Nasser's regime to solve the fundamental problems of industrial growth and population control resulted in the adoption of violent anti-Zionism and anticolonialism as a basis for political slogans which were designed to appease the criticisms of the alienated political masses. The continuity of Nasser's charismatic leadership (Dekmejian, 1971) in the face of political failures required mass extremism. The starting point for an analysis of negative criticism of Third World nationalism must, however, centre on the Actonian publications of Elie Kedourie.

Kedourie's criticisms of nationalist ideology are motivated by what he takes to be the false claims of nationalists about nationalism, and the equally misguided interpretations of the economic causes of nationalist movements by Marxists. Nationalist movements are not in any straightforward sense a direct, indigenous response to attacks on nationhood by alien colonialism. On the contrary, nationalism, in Kedourie's view, is 'a doctrine invented in Europe at the beginning of the nineteenth century' (1960, p. 9) which was imported into the Third World by European societies who embarked on a programme of colonial expansion, not because of an economic crisis in the Western economy, but because of political and military rivalry. Nationalism 'pretends to supply a criterion for the determination of the unit proper to enjoy a government exclusively its own' (Kedourie, 1960, p. 9). These nationalist ideologies of the Third World are based on three major assumptions. They have to assume that possessing a nationality is as natural as possessing teeth or red hair and that there are certain natural divisions in humanity along national lines. Nationalists tend to regard struggles for self-determination as a form of 'awakening' of the nation from slumber (Minogue, 1967). Thus, one of the most influential of the early Arab nationalist tracts bears the title *The Arab Awakening* (Antonius, 1938). The second major assumption of nationalist ideology is that each nation can be clearly distinguished by certain empirical features, especially language and religion. Finally, it is assumed that self-government by co-nationals is the only form of legitimate government. Kedourie then attempts to show that these three arguments about the nature of nationalism are logically absurd in order to defend his own view that the best test of government leaders is not whether they happen to speak the same language but whether they are 'corrupt and grasping, or more just and merciful' than some 'alien' government.

The first assumption that nationality is a natural attribute of human beings is quite obviously false. In historical terms, the coincidence of political boundaries with ethnic, linguistic and cultural boundaries has been rare. The political units of human history—tribes, villages, cities and empires—have only uncommonly corresponded to 'nations' (Gellner, 1964). The mosaic model has the virtue, at a low level of empirical generality, of drawing attention to the fact that the Ottoman, Mamluk and Safavi empires were sprawling political entities incorporating a diversity of ethnic and cultural groups.

The idea that, because of their naturalness, nations are easily and readily identified by reference to certain observable .traits is equally suspect. Nations are not so much discovered as created by the labours of the intelligentsia. Kedourie (1970) draws attention to the ways in which nationalist intellectuals have to redefine and rewrite history in order to characterise social development as the awakening of hitherto sleeping nations. Thus, the Ottoman Empire and the empires of North Africa and the Middle East come to be regarded as the political and cultural expression of 'Turks' and 'Arabs'. This reworking of history in terms of self-conscious nations involves subtle changes in the etymology of certain key terms. Originally 'Turk' and 'Arab' referred to rustic peasants without culture or significance, but these terms have to be refashioned and elevated to play a greater historical role. Similarly Bernard Lewis (1961, 1965) has identified important changes in the terms *vatan* (residence) and *millet* (religion) in the nineteenth century which resulted in the equation of *vatan* and nation. It is precisely because of the ethnic and linguistic diversity of Islamic history that common agreements about religion came to play a large part in defining common national characteristics. In order for religion to play a role subservient to the dominant interests of nation building, Islam had to be changed in a number of important ways. The Orientalist argument is that Islam was secularised in the sense that it came to be regarded as a system of personal morality which could provide a basis for secular nationalism. In other words, 'religion' was differentiated from 'politics' in order to serve the nation.

In terms of the third assumption, rule by co-nationals has been the exception rather than the norm. The ruling class of the traditional Islamic empires was composed of Turks, Mongols, Greeks and Albanians (to give them their modern designations) who constituted an 'alien' elite in terms of language, culture and ethnicity in relation to the subordinate Arab classes. Furthermore, a common national identity between rulers and ruled is no guarantee of good government. This fact leads Kedourie to consider a puzzle which is a standard feature of nationalism. The indigenous intelligentsia has been trained and brought up within the traditions of European culture and science which are universalistic, secular and rational. Yet it is precisely this intelligentsia which, in order to create a sense of national identity, is in the forefront of those attempts to revive folk culture, 'primitive' languages, barbaric practices and pre-modern moralities. Kedourie's answer is that intellectuals adhere to nationalism because they are 'marginal men'. They are trained in white/colonial institutions which has the effect of isolating them from their indigenous environment, but, at the same time, they are not completely assimilated by the colonial society. George Antonius and Edward Atiyah, two Christian Arabs who contributed to the rise of Arab nationalism, provide two pertinent illustrations. Both men were educated within British institutions and enjoyed distinguished careers in educational terms. Antonius was an undergraduate at King's College, Cambridge, while Atiyah went to Brasenose, Oxford. Both men failed to achieve administrative and educational posts within the British colonial administration to which they were entitled in terms of their education, experience and seniority. Condemned to fulfil minor administrative duties by virtue of their background, Antonius and Atiyah rejected their initial espousal of British culture and politics and turned to Arab culture as a method of determining their own identity in opposition to British rule.

While Kedourie wants to criticise nationalism on the grounds that it is philosophically invalid, the suggestion that nationalist ideology is the work of frustrated intellectuals and officials from the ranks of the indigenous middle class carries with it the covert implication that nationalist claims can be dismissed as merely the splenetic outpourings of dissatisfied intellectuals. Nationalist ideology is criticised by the imputation of 'bad motives' to marginal intellectuals. This method of attack is clearly illustrated by Kedourie's study of two Islamic reformers, Jamal al-Din al-Afghani and Muhammad 'Abduh (1966). According to Kedourie, these reformist theories are suspect because al-Afghani and 'Abduh posed as men of religion whereas in fact they were political men manipulating the masses through the appeal to religion. In public, al-Afghani and 'Abduh claimed that Islam could come to terms with the modern world only by reforming itself. However, the reformation of Islam merely required a return to the pristine doctrines of the Prophet prior to the period when Islam was subverted by irrational and alien accretions. The true Muslim, in al-Afghani's view, rejected imitation (*taqlid*) of ancestors and espoused independent reasoning (the reopening of the 'gate of *ijtihād*') in the field of law (Keddie, 1968). In private, these reformers believed that Islam, whether reformed or otherwise, was in principle incompatible with rationality and modernity. Islam, however, had an important social and political function in securing the loyalty of the masses to government. This machiavellian commitment to political expediency was clearly illustrated, according to Kedourie, by the notorious exchange between the French philosopher Ernest Renan and al-Afghani in 1883. In his lecture 'L'Islamisme et la science' in the *Journal des Débats* (Renan, 1887), Renan argued that Islam, like any other revealed religion, was reactionary and irrational. In his reply, al-Afghani agreed that Islam had inhibited the progress of science and, like Christianity, belonged to a stage of human evolution which would be replaced ultimately by rationalism. In the interim, the masses would remain emotionally dependent on religion. Kedourie (1965) argues that, while al-Afghani was happy to appear in the role of *Asiatique éclairé* to his European audience, he was more than reluctant to allow the dissemination of these beliefs in Islamic countries where he had a reputation for pious orthodoxy. Kedourie's approach, therefore, is not only to challenge the philosophical basis of nationalist beliefs, but to raise questions about the motivation of nationalist and reformist leaders. Muslim reformers are treated as political agents who hide their 'real' motives under a camouflage of pious orthodoxy (Asad, 1976).

Kedourie's views have been criticised on a number of grounds. Gellner (1964) argues that, whatever the virtues of Kedourie's position as a critique of the *intellectual* content of nationalist claims, it would be a mistake to confuse the sociological significance of nationalism with its logical status. A similar position is taken by Peter Worsley (1964) who notes that by taking nationalist claims at their face value we may miss the sociological point of nationalism which serves a number of critical social needs. These are 'how to realize aspirations, how to overthrow a rejected order, how to live together' (Worsley, 1964, p. 80). In general, these objections amount to saying that Kedourie's liberalism prevents him from grasping the sociological necessity of nationalist beliefs within the context of a struggle for national liberation (Smith, 1971, pp. 12-24). While various critiques of Kedourie's theory are well known, Kedourie remains a powerful influence, directly or indirectly, on the study of the nature and rise of Arab nationalism. This influence operates at two levels. First, there is the general position that, for a number of reasons, Arab nationalism is a defective version of European nationalism. Secondly, Kedourie has established a number of core themes—the centrality of Islamic reform for Arab secular nationalism, the role of 'marginal men' in the formulation of nationalist beliefs, and the ambiguity of the relationship between Western modernisation and anti-colonial nationalism—which continue to dominate sociological discussion of nationalism.

The arguments concerning the intimate relationship between Islamic reform and subsequent secular nationalism are the central feature of contemporary historical studies of Islam and de-colonisation. The Turkish case is instructive in this context (Berkes, 1964). Most accounts of secularisation in Turkey emphasise the superficial and mimetic features of the Kemalist reforms such as the legislation relating to personal dress (the Hat Law of 1925), writing and custom. The general trend of Kemalist legislation was to separate religious education from traditional values and institutions so that Islam could provide a moral basis for a modern, industrial society (Turner, 1974a). The idea that

Islam could perform this sociological function of social solidarity was the central theme of the social philosophy of Ziya Gökalp (Berkes, 1959) whose sociological notions were derived ultimately from Durkheim's views on the collective conscience and nationalism (Mitchell, 1931). The separation of morals and politics is achieved in the name of the reform of Islam which is regarded as a puritan, this-worldly system of rational beliefs. A similar process of secularisation and reform has been detected in other parts of the Middle East and North Africa. These reforms are most obvious in the case of the laws relating to personal status, where monogamy, the rights of women, and rights of divorce are defended by reference to the practices of the Prophet and pristine Islam (Salem, 1965). The reformation of Islam, especially in such developments as the Salafiyya movement, has been treated as a necessary stage in the development of secular nationalism (Abun-Nasr, 1963; Wolf, 1971a, 1971b). This labour of secularisation has been primarily brought about by 'marginal men' and in particular by Christian Arabs whose view of nationalism was necessarily shaped by Western assumptions as they were mediated by missionary institutions in Egypt and the Fertile Crescent (Tibawi, 1963; Haddad, 1970).

These studies of the nature of Arab nationalism have the effect, probably unintentionally, of reinforcing the Orientalist view that nationalism in the Middle East is essentially defective and partial because it has failed to challenge the conventional religiosity of the masses. Arab nationalism remains frozen in its transition from a religious to a secular world. This feature of Arab nationalism also provides a strong contrast to Zionism which is often held to be radical, secular and successful. Thus, Anthony Smith has argued that, by contrast with Jewry, 'Arab society has remained a fundamentally religious community by definition, in which to flaunt agnosticism is socially unacceptable because it undermines the basis of communal life and its raison d'être' (1973, p. 35). With only one exception, that of Egypt, there is no Arab counterpart to the 'step-like transition from religion to nationalism' (Smith, 1973, p. 42) which is characteristic of the Jewish transition to radical national politics. A similar position has been taken by Abbas Kelidar (1975) who notes that, because the political elite was unable to fashion a relevant secular and radical ideology for the Middle East, the elite was forced to attempt the adaptation of traditional Islam to modern conditions, but unfortunately no such adaptation is possible. The trend of these various approaches to the study of Arab nationalism is toward one general conclusion which has been succinctly stated by Vatikiotis, to the effect that, despite a century of Islamic reform, Arab nationalism 'has yet to produce an Arab polity' because it has yet to change 'an old political culture (Islamic, dynastic, tribal, military-autocratic) and with it a basically traditional society' (Vatikiotis, 1971, p. 23).

The idea that nationalism is a necessary stage in the transition from traditional to modern society and that the Western experience of nationalism and nation-states has global significance can be challenged on the grounds that it presupposes an idealist and historicist view of empirical history (Asad, 1975). The demolition of the Orientalist view of nationalism by Marxism, however, presupposes either that Marxism itself possesses a coherent theory of nationalism, or that 'nationalism' can be shown to be an ideological concept which cannot be constituted as a proper object of scientific discourse. The first possibility is doubtful and the second possibility may well solve the 'problem' of nationalism by showing it to be false; but this very achievement only serves to throw further doubt on higher order concepts, like the Marxist concept of the 'superstructure'. However, before embarking on the issue of a Marxist theory of nationalism, we have to take notice of the fact that there are Hegelian versions of Marxism which tend to converge with an Orientalist understanding of Arab nationalism. It will be necessary, therefore, to return to Avineri's account of Zionism in order to illustrate this convergence of Hegelianism and Orientalism.

Avineri's views on the differences between Arab and Jewish nationalism have evolved out of his synthesis of a pot-pourri of nineteenth century philosophies, with Hegel, Moses Hess and Ber Borochov providing the main ingredients (Avineri, 1962; Berlin, 1970). Whereas Jewry was able to make a 'step-like' progression from religion to politics and eventually to a fundamental social revolution, Islam has achieved only a superficial political nationalism which still has significant religious roots. In Avineri's analysis, the very essence of Islam makes it incompatible with democratic, radical nationalism. Islamic society is the product of the Arab *Conquista* of the Middle East, and because Islamic politics and culture were shaped by a military elite the idea of opposition to military rule as a matter of principle 'is quite lacking in Arab society' (Avineri, 1976, p. 119). Since the military elite held commercial activity in disdain, trade was carried on by minority groups with the result that a middle class as the main agent of nationalist politics never developed. By contrast, Diaspora Jewry possessed a fully developed middle class which could give expression to Jewish nationalist sentiment. The downward social mobility of middle class Jewish settlers in Palestine gave Zionism a strong critical and socialist complexion. The post-colonial Arab states represent a continuity of the old Islamic societies based on military rule. The ideologies of Arab nationalism and socialism do not correspond to a reorganisation of social values and social structure. The most ferocious and determined opposition to Western rule came not from secular nationalists but from various fundamentalist religious groups—Abd el Kader in North Africa, the Mahdi in Sudan and the Sanusi of Cyrenaica (Evans-Pritchard, 1949). In modern times, the principal leaders of nationalist, anti-Western movements—Hajj Amin al-Husseini, Colonel Gadafi, President Boumedienne—have all turned to 'Islam as their basic ideological framework' (Avineri, 1976, p. 108).

My objections to the accounts of Arab nationalism presented by
Avineri, Smith and Vatikiotis are based neither on a disputation as to the
'facts' of the case nor on a politically motivated desire to defend Arab
nationalism against a liberal critique. My objection is more fundamental
since, throughout this discussion of Orientalism, it is necessary to
criticise the basic mode of analysis of Orientalism which produces these
'facts' and political opinions regarding the nature of Middle East social
formations. These assumptions are that history is an unfolding essence
which passes through certain necessary stages under the dominance of
necessary classes (especially the middle class) and that Western history
stands in a privileged relationship to Eastern history. The difficulty is
that on this specific issue of nationalism the production of a Marxist
critique of the sociology of nationalism is inhibited by the absence of an
articulate Marxist theory of nationalism.

There appears to be widespread agreement among Marxists and non-
Marxists that the failure to develop a coherent account of nationalism
represents one of Marxism's most damaging theoretical weaknesses. This
difficulty has been referred to as a 'mistake' (Gellner, 1964, p. 172), as
'cynical' (Minogue, 1967, p. 143) and as a 'great historical failure'
(Nairn, 1975, p. 3). Part of the problem is that Marx and Engels left no
clear *theoretical* guideline for conceptualising the phenomenon of
nationalism and hence 'no explanation of how to deal, theoretically, with
the ethnic divisions of mankind when confronted with divisions based on
class' (Kolakowski, 1974, p. 48). The consequence has been that Marxist
positions on questions of nationalism have been frequently dictated by
matters of immediate political strategy rather than analytical penetration. Official attitudes to the National Question evolved through a series
of crises. Within the context of the social cleavages of the Austro-
Hungarian Empire, the Austro-Marxist school attempted to apply
Marxist perspectives and approaches to imperialism and nationalism as
these phenomena were manifested within the specific conditions of
capitalism in Austria. The major contribution in this area was provided
by the youthful Otto Bauer in his *The Nationalities Question and Social
Democracy* (in Marx-Studien, 11, Vienna, 1907) in which Bauer offered a
general analysis of the genesis and composition of nations. The First
World War shattered the illusion that the working classes 'have no
country' (Lichtheim, 1970; Berki, 1971). Whereas Lenin had approached
the National Question as a matter of strategy in arousing revolutionary
consciousness, Rosa Luxemburg had attacked the whole notion of 'the
Nation' as a bourgeois concept which had the effect of blurring class
antagonisms. Under Stalin's auspices, the policy on nationalism was
developed under the banner of 'Socialism in one country' in the 1920s
and in the interests of Russian nationalism in the 1930s. The trend in the
post-Second World War period, starting with Yugoslavia's 'own road'

and developing under the influence of anti-colonial liberation movements, has been to favour the idea of 'self-governing communities'. These strategic decisions over particular nationalist movements do not, however, resolve the theoretical issue as to whether 'national interest' is compatible with 'class interest'.

It is sometimes suggested that Marxist views on nationalism (for example, the notion that nationalism is basically an effect of colonial struggles) are too simple to fit the complexity of the history and content of diverse nationalist movements (Smith, 1969, 1971). The problem, however, is not to attempt to match up theory with the facts of nationalism since in epistemological terms this is to assume that 'facts' are theory-neutral. The search for typologies of increasing sophistication to describe the complexity of the real world will not produce any theoretical solution. By recognising that the crucial issue is whether 'nationalism' is a proper object of scientific discourse, Sami Zubaida (1977) is able to provide an alternative to the search for a sociological typology of nationalisms. A general theory of nationalism would have to conceptualise 'nationalism' as 'a unitary general phenomenon, perhaps with particular variants and sub-types', while a sociological theory of nationalism would have to postulate 'common social structures and processes which underlie the ideological/political phenomena' (Zubaida, 1977, p. 7). What sociological theories of nationalism have in common is that they attribute nationalism to some global, historical process (modernisation, industrialisation or capitalist development) and identify a number of primary social classes or strata (usually the intellectuals) as the bearers of nationalist beliefs. Zubaida attacks the notion of a general theory of nationalism on two major issues. First, the so-called global waves of industrialisation, modernisation or capitalist development do not have uniform effects. For example, capitalist relations of production can be established in a society on the basis of archaic, non-capitalist relations of exploitation. The precise nature of the consequences of social development hinge on specific conjunctures within given social formations so that no general theory of these effects on a global scale is possible. Secondly, the theory that the middle class, or more specifically the intellectual stratum within the middle class, is crucial in formulating nationalist beliefs and organising the early stages of nationalist struggles assumes that the 'middle class' is a universal category and that comparisons between the middle classes of various social formations are legitimate. Social classes, however, are defined in terms of the relations of production and these in turn presuppose a rigorous specification of modes of production. It is not possible to accept the vague generalisations about the role of the middle class in sociological theories of nationalism because these theories do not provide any adequate analysis of the specific combinations of relations of production in post-colonial and industrial social formations. On the basis of these two arguments, it follows that 'nationalism' is not a valid 'unitary object of sociological investigation' (Zubaida, 1977, p. 10).

While the sociological analysis of 'nationalism' is not a viable enterprise and while it is not a problem for Marxist theory to produce a definition of 'nation' and 'nationalism', Zubaida argues that 'nationalism' is to be treated as a crucial problem for political practice. The classical Marxist literature does not produce or attempt to produce a general theory of nationalism, but we do find in Lenin's work a clear principle that socialists should support democratic movements of national self-determination and oppose movements which are directed towards nationalist expansion and domination of others. Although in my view Zubaida sets off on the right track, I have three objections to his conclusion that 'nationalism' is a practical, not theoretical problem. First, his position entails a form of disguised empiricism since what he achieves is not so much a demonstration of the theoretical incoherence of sociologies of nationalism but rather a demonstration that a *general* theory cannot cope with the empirical specificity of particular nationalist movements. The world is too complex to be subsumed under general categories like 'middle class', 'modernisation' or 'nationalism'. The Leninist view that the heart of Marxism is the concrete analysis of concrete situations is an empiricist distinction between theory and the concrete, and furthermore is not a particularly illuminating comment on Marxist methods of analysis. Secondly, Zubaida's argument, which assumes a clear distinction between theory and practice, cannot provide an account of what role theory might play in Marxist analysis as such. Are all the classical problems—class struggle, capitalist crises, revolution, consciousness—in the end not problems of theory but of practice? Such a position is not far removed from Weber's notion that sociological theory has no privileged status in relation to political practice since knowledge of the world (what is) cannot tell us how to behave (what we ought to do). Thirdly, an appeal to political practice and calculation is no real guide to deciding which nationalist movements should win the support of socialists. The situation is particularly difficult when two or more nationalist movements are in a state of open conflict, for example Jewish versus Palestinian nationalisms.

An alternative solution would be to argue that 'nationalism' is a commonsense, quasi-scientific term which operates within an ideological discourse and which has to be transformed in order to operate within a scientific realm of analysis. This approach would attempt to resolve the apparent contradiction between 'national interest' and 'class interest' via the theory of ideology or, more generally, of the superstructure. Unfortunately, this sort of solution to the ideological concept of 'nationalism' runs into notorious difficulties in connection with the relationship between base and superstructure (Williams, 1973; Hirst, 1976).

The development of a Marxist theory of the superstructure has been hampered by the fact that Marx and Engels adhered to at least three theories of ideology, or, to be more precise, three theories of belief can be adduced from Marx and Engels' publications. These are (a) the appearance/reality theory, (b) a social class theory of belief and (c) a mode of production theory. While the theory of alienation, fetishised relationships and mystification can produce sophisticated analyses of ideology, there are a number of difficulties which centre on Marx's use of various metaphors and analogies to explain the nature of ideological belief in capitalist social formations (Geras, 1971; Mepham, 1972). In its vulgar form, this particular theory results in the notion that 'nationalist beliefs' are a form of false consciousness, but that is merely a description of a state of affairs rather than an explanation. The most conventional form of Marxist analysis of beliefs is to reduce belief systems to class interests; for example, capitalist beliefs in exchange and individualism are held to be beliefs which are appropriate to the bourgeoisie (Goldmann, 1973). In *The Condition of the Working Class in England* (Engels, 1968) and in the Preface to the *Contribution to the Critique of Political Economy* (Marx, 1971), we find the theory that 'social being determines consciousness', which has been conventionally interpreted as asserting that 'social class determines consciousness'. Each social class grasps its experience of material conditions in the form of beliefs which are unique to that class. In capitalism, the working class has 'other thoughts and ideals, other customs and moral principles, a different religion and other politics than those of the bourgeoisie' (Engels, 1968, p. 124). The superstructure of a social formation is thus composed of the different belief systems of separate social classes. This view of ideology is not easily reconciled with the other conventional class theory of beliefs which claims that the ideas of 'the ruling class are in every epoch the ruling ideas' (Marx and Engels, 1974, p. 64). Since the dominant class controls mental production and has a monopoly of the distribution of beliefs, it is able to ensure the incorporation of the working class. This theory implies that the superstructure will be a relatively homogeneous structure integrated around the beliefs of the dominant class. Rosa Luxemburg's view that nationalism, or the idea of 'nation above class', is a component of bourgeois ideology which has the function of undermining the force of economic class interest, has to presume some form of 'ruling ideas' thesis. Unfortunately, the 'ruling ideas' theory has to assume that the dominant class owns the means of mental production and controls an adequate apparatus for the dissemination of beliefs, and that the working class is a *tabula rasa* or at least highly susceptible to ideological contamination. These assumptions are all questionable. In empirical terms, most of the evidence suggests that in feudalism and capitalism the peasantry and working class were not, or were only partially, incorporated within the dominant ideology (Parkin, 1972; Mann, 1973; Goodridge, 1975).

The third type of theory of ideology in Marx attempts to conceptualise belief systems not as class beliefs but as specific conditions of modes of production. This theory can be elaborated on the basis of Marx's comments in *Capital* (Vol. 1, 1970, pp. 85-6) where he observes that 'the mode of production of material life' determines all forms of social, political and intellectual life in capitalist society where 'material interests preponderate, but not for the middle ages, in which Catholicism, nor for Athens and Rome, where politics, reigned supreme'. This quotation from Marx is used by Althusser (Althusser and Balibar, 1970) and by Poulantzas (1973) as a method of resolving some of the difficulties which have surrounded the claim that the economy determines the superstructure only in 'the last instance'. The economic base determines which of the three structures (economic, political and ideological) of the mode of production will be dominant. Thus, in slavery the economy determines the dominant role of the political structure; in feudalism, the dominance of ideology. While the notion of dominance remains vague in the work of Althusser and Poulantzas, Hindess and Hirst (1975) provide a far more rigorous interpretation of Marx's commentary by arguing that in the FMP the ideological/political structure is a condition of existence of the mode of production. That is, the separation of the peasantry from partial control over the means of production and the extraction of a surplus requires the existence of extra-economic means of coercion. The super-structure specifies the base by securing the conditions of existence of the mode of production.

The point of this convoluted note on Marxist theories of ideology is not to provide a synoptic summary of the field but merely to make some observations on the difficulty of replacing the Orientalist/sociological treatment of nationalism by a Marxist analysis. It is traditionally thought that nationalism is a problem for Marxism because of the apparent conflict between nation/national interest and class/class interest. One solution to this traditional issue would be to show that 'nationalism' is a quasi-scientific concept which could be transformed and reanalysed in terms of a theory of the superstructure. Such a transformation is delayed by the more basic difficulty of providing a coherent theory of ideology. Although the concept of 'false consciousness' and the 'ruling ideas' thesis lead to somewhat 'vulgar' positions in relation to nationalist beliefs, recent attempts (Hindess and Hirst, 1975) to provide a theory of ideological/political structures as conditions of existence of modes of production are theoretically more promising. For example, instead of arguing that nationalist beliefs correspond to the class interests of the petty bourgeoisie or to the intelligentsia as a stratum of the new petty bourgeoisie, the endeavour would be to conceptualise the ideology of nationalism as a set of beliefs and practices which corresponds to some special features of the modes of production of post-colonial social formations. One of the pressing problems of the post-colonial state is to give symbolic expression at the level of ideology to the unity of the social formation in a situation where the territorial boundaries of 'society' have been arbitrarily established by a colonial administration (Saul, 1974). In this case, the idea of 'nation above class' would correspond, not directly to class interests, but to the political/ideological needs of the state which enjoys relative autonomy from contending classes and from the economic base. The possibility of explaining the presence or absence of nationalist beliefs and nationalist movements by reference to specific conditions of the modes of production of colonial and post-colonial social formations does, however, bring us full circle. The difficulty of providing a demolition of the Orientalist view of nationalism via an analysis of the superstructure turns out to be contingent on the difficulty of providing a coherent theory of the modes of production in colonial and post-colonial countries as an alternative to the mosaic model of Islam.

Despite the difficulties which are entailed by an adequate theoretical formulation of the relationship between ideological structures, the mode of production and the class struggle, it can be said that Marxism has achieved a relative demolition of the Orientalist view that Arab nationalism is a defective variety of 'real' nationalism. Marxism achieves this partial demolition on a number of levels. In order to demonstrate the defective qualities of Arab nationalism, Orientalism is forced to assume that there is such a thing as *the* Western model of social development (the 'bourgeois revolution', secularisation and radical democratisation) and that this model has global relevance. This model is problematic because, for example, the capitalist development of Britain, Germany and France assumed radically different forms according to the specific conditions which obtained in those societies in terms of their different and complex structuring of modes of production (Poulantzas, 1973). This 'fact' about the specificity of the conditions of capitalist development has not passed unnoticed in more enlightened sociological circles (Moore, 1966). The second front of the Orientalist attack on Arab nationalism is to show through accounts of the biographies of individual Arab nationalists that nationalist beliefs are the direct product of 'bad' motives. In order to deal with this position, it is not necessary to get involved in disputes as to whether al-Afghani 'really' was a cynical manipulator of pious masses. It is sufficient to note that the Orientalist position has to reduce ideological structures and practices to an account of the biography of the beliefs of individuals. In short, Orientalists treat the problem of ideology as a problem of intellectual history in order to demonstrate that the 'failure' of Arab nationalism can be traced back to a 'failure' of Arab ideologues. Ideology, however, is not a matter concerning the beliefs of individual subjects but a concept referring to ideological structures and practices which insert subjects into places within the relations of production and which guarantee the reproduction of those relations by securing their conditions of existence (such as the separation of manual and mental labour) (Althusser, 1971).

While the Western model of secularisation does not stand in a privileged *theoretical* relationship to an ideal type of 'Islamic society', it is the case that under colonialism Western capitalism possessed a privileged relationship to dependent Middle East societies in economic and political terms. The rise of Arab nationalism and its specific characteristics must be sought, consequently, not at the level of human biography, but in terms of 'the evolving structures of a specific precapitalist society forcibly subordinated to a world market system' (Asad, 1975, p. 94). Arab nationalism is thus an ideological expression of that conjuncture of economic and political forces, and corresponds to the complex struggle and alliance of social classes within those dependent societies. Because Orientalists have in general perceived the opposition of nationalists to the imperial order through Actonian spectacles, they have been unable to recognise the liberating features of the nationalist struggle. These liberating dimensions of nationalist opposition are limited and frustrated by the very contradictions of colonialism to which nationalist beliefs give expression. That is, nationalist opposition is frustrated by 'the nationalist suppression of the class struggle' (Asad, 1975, p. 96). However, in order to demonstrate that this is the case, we have to be able to demonstrate the validity of the theory that 'national interest' is subordinate to, or derivative from 'class interest'. This demonstration is frustrated by the indecision of Marxists as to whether the National Question is a problem of strategy (Lenin) or primarily a question of theory (Rosa Luxemburg). For those who believe that strategic and theoretical issues in Marxism cannot be separated, there still remains the problem of whether the explanation of ideological structures is to be sought at the level of the concrete struggle of social classes or at the more formal and theoretical level of the conditions of existence of modes of production. The resolution of this final problem depends on the provision of a theory which will resolve the apparent contradiction between two Marxist propositions: either 'revolutions are the effects of class struggles in concrete conjunctures' or 'revolutions are the effects of the transformation of modes of production'. It is because of these unsolved theoretical issues that I regard the Marxist demolition of the Orientalist view of the defectiveness of Arab nationalism as partial rather than total.

5

Revolutions: Modes of Production and Social Classes

We have now considered the various ways by which Orientalism attempts to make a stark contrast between the history and social structure of Western societies and Islamic societies. Western history is dynamic; Middle East societies are stagnant before colonial penetration. Western societies were based on some form of class stratification which is regarded as a condition of industrial development; Islamic societies are based on a mosaic of social groups. In the West, the critical transformation from feudal/religious culture to industrial/secular culture required the services of an autonomous, commercial middle class; in the Islamic Middle East, such a class was missing. This analysis, therefore, is an atavistic example of the ideal type comparisons which were common to most nineteenth century theories of social change. For example, Herbert Spencer's distinction between 'Militant Society' and 'Industrial Society' resembles the Orientalist world-view. In 'Militant Society', the need for military efficiency precludes individual initiative in the field of business and the existence of democratic rights. 'Industrial Society' represented the utilitarian paradise of social harmony, individualism and industrial growth (Burrow, 1970). In more general terms, the Orientalist's ideal typical contrast between East and West is simply a variant of the political theory of Oriental Despotism (Koebner, 1951; Venturi, 1963). These diverse elements within the Orientalist theory of Islamic society turn out to depend upon one fundamental claim, namely, that Middle East societies have not been galvanised by successful bourgeois revolutions and thus are caught in a sociological limbo between 'Militant Society' and 'Industrial Society'. The crucial absence in the evolution of Middle East societies is the revolutionary restructuring of thought, social organisation and political institutions.

The No Revolutions thesis is the prominent feature of most commentaries on traditional and contemporary Middle East societies. Avineri's interpretation of the nature of the militarised Arab societies is based on the fundamental premise that these societies have not experienced genuine *social* revolutions but merely political *coups d'état* and palace revolutions. I. William Zartman finds it surprising that little research has been undertaken on revolutions in the Middle East, but the surprise disappears when one realises that 'there have been few violent, transforming sociopolitical upheavals in the area' (1976, p. 284). There is a wide consensus that the political history of the Middle East is dominated by the military take-over rather than mass revolutions because Arab populations have a preference for 'strong regimes' rather than for the uncertainty of radical democratic politics (Khadduri, 1953). In recent research, the most potent expression of the No Revolutions thesis has been given in a collection of essays with the title *Revolution in the Middle East* (Vatikiotis, 1972). The central argument of this study of revolutions is provided by Vatikiotis in his Introduction where he claims that 'struggles for independence and radical movements in the Middle East, *coups d'état*, insurrections and rebellions so far do not constitute revolutions' (1972, pp. 12-13). In Vatikiotis' terms, a revolution is primarily a form of political action against the *status quo*; such political activity presupposes a revolutionary ideology which contains within it a radical, total alternative to existing social arrangements. Furthermore, the requirements of a revolutionary struggle are strong political organisation, subjective commitment to revolutionary alternatives and some form of mass political involvement and participation. The revolutions of Western society and those of Russia and China were based on a tradition of revolutionary culture and political organisation which transformed oppositional sentiments into full-blooded revolutionary politics. By contrast, the revolts and rebellions of the Middle East are predominantly non-revolutionary responses to European colonial intervention by the 'educated official classes'. These revolts have not been class struggles organised on the basis of an indigenous political ideology for the purpose of radical, post-colonial reconstruction.

The reorganisations of social structure in the Middle East in modern times have been brought about by the intervention of the state which is seen by Vatikiotis as an instrument of bureaucratic, military classes. This situation provides a clear contrast to the history of Western societies. The revolutionary culture of Europe and North America has its roots in classical Greek society, especially the philosophy of Stoicism, 'the universal humanism of Christianity' and, more recently, the natural law tradition. What these cultural roots provide is an oppositional culture which is founded on the principle that citizens have a clear right to resist bad government. The major turning point in Western political philosophy was the French Revolution which gave a new significance to the meaning of 'revolution'. The French philosophers came to use the term to signify a massive change in the organisation of a society which has been brought about by the conscious activity of human beings.

One of the principal aims of the Vatikiotis collection of essays is to establish the fact that the absence of Arab revolutions is a result of the absence of an indigenous concept of revolution. Bernard Lewis (1972) considers a number of Arabic terms which have been pressed into the service of describing revolutions and political uprisings—*dawla, fitna, bid'a, thawra, bagha*—from the period of the fall of the Umayyad Caliphate to the arrival of socialist regimes in Egypt, Syria and Iraq. Most of these terms have strong religious connotations since they refer to actions or beliefs which are deviations from religious orthodoxy. Like Vatikiotis, Lewis arrives at the conclusion that the political right to oppose bad government is 'alien to Islamic thought. Instead, there is an Islamic doctrine of the duty to resist impious government, which in early times was of crucial significance' (Lewis, 1972, p. 33). This right to resist impious rulers was an extremely limited right for two reasons. No clear criteria were ever developed by jurists by which governmental impiety could be tested, and furthermore no apparatus was evolved by which these rights could be adequately enforced against an existing political authority. In Islamic history, according to Lewis, the duty of obedience had ascendancy over the right to resist and this contributed to the social conformity and political quietism which is the hallmark of traditional Islamic society. Because religion and politics are 'inextricably inter-mingled' in Islamic civilisations, religious dissent always carried with it the threat of serious disruption for the social order. To protect society from these social disorders (*fitna*) and departure from orthodox custom (*bid'a*), conformity was to be bought at any cost. The religious principle of resistance ('There is no obedience in sin') was consequently over-shadowed by the more pressing requirements of political order and social stability.

It could be objected that, while the medieval Islamic period may have had these characteristics, the nineteenth century was a major turning point in the spread of opposition and revolt throughout North Africa and the Middle East. It is possible to list a number of political confron-tations—the 'Urabi revolt of 1882, the Egyptian revolutions of 1919 and 1952, the Damascus massacre of 1860, the Syrian revolt against French rule in 1925—which could be regarded as revolutionary struggles. Against this possibility, Albert Hourani argues that these social move-ments 'may have been feuds rather than revolutions' (1972, p. 67). One reason for taking this position is that the struggles for political power in the Middle East have been traditionally conducted in terms of a 'Politics of Notables' (Hourani, 1968). In the provincial centres of the Ottoman Empire, administration and government were controlled by Ottoman officials, while the mobilisation of public support was the work of local notables. The political activities of the notables were focused on securing the support of city mobs, craft guilds and religious leaders, dealing with rivals and securing influence with the Ottoman officialdom. The object of this 'Politics of Notables' was not to overthrow an existing social order or to create a new system of government but to 'preserve or make stable the balance between local governor and local leaders on which provincial society depended' (Hourani, 1972, p. 67). The uprisings and political struggles of the nineteenth century were primarily feuds between rival groups of notables for political influence. In the second half of the twentieth century with the disappearance of alien political rule, the 'Politics of Notables' collapses and is replaced by new political struggles. Political actors who are inside the system compete for access to the benefits distributed by the central bureaucracy, while those on the out-side aim for the overthrow of the 'government, using the only method which seems likely to be effective: the armed forces' (Hourani, 1972, p. 72). Revolution, of a sort, now becomes for the first time a genuine possibility.

If the revolts of the nineteenth century were simply feuds between factions within the noble stratum, then the 'revolutions' of the period of decolonisation turn out to be military take-overs. For example, the political upheavals of the Maghreb also fail to satisfy the criteria of 'real revolutions' which have been established by Vatikiotis and his col-leagues. The Algerian Revolution was the work of a 'small number of leaders' who were able to mobilise the mass of the population but this elite has 'lulled them since independence with hopes, slogans and formal demonstrations' (Tourneau *et al.*, 1972, p. 97). Instead of developing a revolutionary ideology based upon the centrality and necessity of class conflict, the military and political elites of the Maghreb have advocated religious conceptions of communal harmony and development without social confrontation. The socialism of the Maghreb represents a continu-ity with the past since 'the altruistic qualities which the building of socialism demands from its citizens are the very qualities of Islam' (Tourneau *et al.*, 1972, p. 109). By these arguments, the No Revolutions thesis is defended against any possible refutation. Classical Islam had no right of resistance; the uprisings of the Ottoman period were feuds; the revolutions of the twentieth century were military coups which ended in the betrayal of socialism.

My objections to the No Revolutions thesis will fall into three sections. It is possible to throw serious doubt upon this argument, even in its own epistemological and theoretical terms of reference, by raising empirical questions about its characterisation of Western history. At a different level, the argument can be criticised by illustrating the assumptions which lie behind its view of Middle East societies and by showing that the argument is a species of the Oriental Despotism tradition of analysis. Finally, as in the case of 'nationalism', I wish to argue that the concept of 'revolution' is an imprecise, quasi-scientific concept which requires con-siderable theoretical criticism and elaboration. This concluding criticism of the Orientalist view of revolution, however, leads us into certain tradi-tional difficulties in Marxism as to whether revolutions are the effects of transformations of modes of production or whether they are effects of class struggle.

The contrast between European and Middle East culture in terms of revolutionary traditions is based, especially in the case of Lewis' article, on the assumption that it is possible to identify *the* Western principle of a right to resist bad government. It is difficult to see how Christian political philosophy and institutions could give rise to such a tradition. The Christian principle of 'rendering unto Caesar' suggests a form of political quietism parallel to Muslim fears about *fitna*. In the medieval period, the conflict over the nature of royal power gave rise to two contradictory theories of kingship in Christendom. According to the theocratic principle, the king received his power from and was responsible to God. The alternative view was that the king received his power from the people and consequently had to pay attention to their demands. From the Merovingian period, the descending theocratic principle was dominant and with the rise of the absolutist monarchies the notions concerning the sacramental nature of rulership evolve toward a fully fledged doctrine of the divine right of kings. Political slogans like 'The king can do no wrong' or 'No writ runs against the king' or 'No bishops, no king' hardly lend support to Lewis' view of the right to resist in Western political life. Even Reformation theology gave very limited scope to the idea that opposition to sinful government was legitimate. In Calvinism the obligation to defend the faith against the intrusion of secular government was closely defined by properly instituted religious authorities (Wolin, 1961). In the modern period, while the argument that Methodism actually saved capitalism from working class violence is obviously contentious, there is little doubt that Methodism and the Protestant sects played a generally conservative role in British politics (Turner and Hill, 1975).

In *the* Western doctrine of the right to resist bad government, Lewis must have in mind the secular tradition of European political thought, especially the theory of a social contract from Hobbes to the Utilitarians. Unfortunately, this particular tradition also placed very severe limitations on the scope of individual freedoms and rights of opposition. Hobbes presented a choice to rational man between anarchy with liberty (the state of nature) and security without freedom (civil society). In Rousseau's philosophy there is an attempt to free men from personal dependence, but social freedom is based on the surrender of individual rights (Charvet, 1974). The liberal tradition appears to offer a genuine commitment to personal liberties and freedom of conscience, but on inspection this particular branch of the Western political tradition also turns out to be suspect. From Malthus through Bentham to J. S. Mill, the liberal/Utilitarian tradition was built around a set of specific anxieties— fear of nature and population growth, fear of economic and social stagnation, fear of the working class in the reformed parliament (Wolin, 1961). In order to protect themselves from these potential disasters, liberal theorists had to hedge individual freedoms around with a variety of institutional restrictions. The exterior claims about equality and freedom were facades which masked an inner pessimism about man and society (Lichtman, 1970). The right to resist was an ideological right not against bad government but against illegitimate government and the difficulties of defining 'legitimacy' in political terms do not appear to be any less complex than those associated with the Islamic idea of 'impious' government. In short, *the* Western political tradition does not provide a clear, automatic right to resist bad government.

By inviting us to consider the absence of revolutions in the Middle East, the No Revolutions thesis thereby obscures the real kernel of its theory, namely, the presence of a revolutionary tradition in the West which presents itself as a unitary object of analysis. The bourgeois revolution is regarded as the crucial factor in the modernisation of Western politics, technology and society. The thesis has, therefore, to assume that the effects of bourgeois revolutions are uniform; empirically, there is little justification for this assumption. As Poulantzas (1973) clearly demonstrates, while the transition from feudalism to capitalism presents certain common features, there is no such thing as the typical model of the 'bourgeois revolution'. Although the French Revolution did demolish the *ancien régime*, it also had the peculiar effect of increasing the political and economic significance of the peasantry by the legalisation of smallholdings. The post-revolutionary structure of rural France had the consequence of delaying capitalist development in the first half of the nineteenth century. This situation led Marx to the conclusion that the French Revolution was a precocious political tragedy which failed to revolutionise the mode of production and which was reproduced in the farce of 1848 (Marx, 1973).

The case of Germany is also problematic for the argument presented by Vatikiotis and Lewis. German political and economic development was brought about 'from above' by a state apparatus which was controlled by a feudal Junker class which excluded the industrial bourgeoisie from political power in exchange for an advantageous tariff system and which intensified pre-capitalist forms of exploitation in the large estates of east Germany. As another illustration, the 'peculiarities of the English' (Anderson, 1964) argument is a fatal stumbling block for the view of the 'bourgeois revolution' which is implied in the No Revolutions thesis. The capitalisation of English agriculture created a capitalist land-owning class in the countryside before the emergence of an industrial bourgeois class, so that in England the dominance of the CMP was not accompanied by any open class struggle between the land-owning aristocracy and the urban bourgeoisie. Further illustrations are hardly necessary. The point of these observations is that there is no *necessary* connection between violent revolution and capitalist development or, in Lewis' terms, there is no *necessary* connection between democracy and industrialisation. On the contrary, the dictatorships of Germany, Italy and Spain were instrumental in the triumph of capitalism by accelerating the concentration of industrial capital and the penetration of agriculture by capitalist relations of production.

In terms of its primary assumptions, the No Revolutions thesis bears all the marks of Orientalism and its historical ancestor, Oriental Despotism. The thesis attempts to discover certain ideal typical factors or essences which will serve to demarcate one homogeneous entity ('the West') from some other timeless entity ('Islamic society'). The thesis has certain superficial sociological trappings in its search for an independent middle class and its characterisation of Ottoman institutions, but the thesis is primarily idealistic. The essential differences between 'the West' and 'Islamic society' are located in religious beliefs, political theories, attitudes of mind and legal notions. These idealist and essentialist assumptions are clearly illustrated in the fact that 'revolution' is defined in commonsense terms as a *political* activity. Thus, Hourani accepts a dictionary definition of 'revolution' as the 'complete overthrow of the established government in any country or state by those who were previously subject to it' (*Shorter Oxford English Dictionary*). Given the narrow conception of revolution and revolutionary struggle in Vatikiotis' *Revolution in the Middle East*, it is difficult to see why a number of political struggles in the Middle East could not count as 'revolutionary'. These would include: the revolutionary struggles in the Gulf (Halliday, 1974), the Palestinian resistance (Aruri, 1970), the Algerian revolution, the Palestinian revolt of 1936-9 (Jankowski, 1973), the Saudi revolution (Edens, 1974) or even the Libyan case (First, 1974). These candidates and others are excluded simply because the whole conception of 'revolution' in the No Revolutions thesis is arbitrary.

Dictionary definitions of 'revolution' will not solve the problem of elementary classification since dictionaries are themselves merely systematisations of common usage and catalogues of ideological terms. While the Orientalist's enterprise of understanding 'revolution' through philology and etymology is less than adequate, the attempts by sociologists and political scientists to come to terms with 'revolutions' have not been obviously successful. As in the case of 'nationalism', the sociology of revolutions has produced descriptive typologies and paradigms rather than explanations (Brinton, 1965; Eckstein, 1965; Stone, 1965; Dunn, 1972; Kramnick, 1972) or sociology has descended into psychologism (Davies, 1962). In order to offer a Marxist alternative to these commonsense approaches to 'revolution', it is important to clear the ground of an initial obstacle. This is to recognise that the theory of the AMP as it appears in Marx and Engels' journalism is a No Revolutions theory. Asiatic society is static and its political history is a matter of circulating dynastic elites rather than class struggles and social transformation. In abandoning the ideological employment of the AMP, we also have to reject the whole enterprise of making essentialist contrasts between 'the

West' and 'Arab society' or, even worse, between 'Christendom' and 'Islam'. I have already indicated the absurdity of claims about *the* Western revolutionary tradition and about a uniform 'bourgeois revolution'. Rather than attempting to make specious comparisons between 'bourgeois revolutions' in the seventeenth century, and the political conflicts of the Middle East in the twentieth century, the task is to understand the specific nature, crises and transformations of the modes of production of post-colonial social formations which provide the general conditions for the predominance of military coups in the struggle for control of the state apparatus. It is thus a specific set of conditions in post-colonial, dependent social formations which gives rise to the military take-over rather than an eternal essence of Islam which constantly reproduces the same social and political structures of 'Islamic society'.

While there are certain difficulties involved in the concept of a 'colonial mode of production', Jairus Banaji's theoretical formulation of the specificity of the post-colonial situation provides an important starting point for the analysis of the military/political crisis of dependent social formations. The primary point at the theoretical level which Banaji (1972) wishes to establish is that a distinction has to be made between relations of exploitation (serfdom, wage labour, slavery), relations of production (the 'historically determined form which particular relations of exploitation assume') and forces of production. This distinction is made in order to demonstrate that the CMP, for example, cannot be defined in terms of the existence of wage labour. The importance of this observation is to show that in the colonies it was typically the case that the spread of capitalist relations of production had the effect of extending and intensifying pre-capitalist, archaic forms of labour organisation and relations of exploitation. In the colonies, capitalism installed a 'retrograde logic' of thwarted primitive accumulation and industrial backwardness. The incorporation of the colonies into the world economy does not 'modernise' these social formations but typically conserves pre-capitalist modes of production and intensifies archaic relations of exploitation while simultaneously retarding the expansion of the home market and indigenous capitalist industry. We can summarise the principal economic features of colonial social formations: '(i) by a retarded development of capitalist production relations in agriculture, hence by a low productivity of peasant labour and stagnant output levels; (ii) by a structure of industry whose backward and one-sided character sprang directly from the policies of delayed primitive accumulation; (iii) by a concentration of exports on the products of agriculture' (Banaji, 1973). The colonial process of industrialisation, where it does take place, further intensifies these peculiarities. In class terms, these features of colonial economies are associated with a slow development of an industrial proletariat, the predominance of the peasantry employed as seasonal wage labourers, the absence of an industrial capitalist class and finally the growing importance of the new petty bourgeoisie.

If these characteristics specify the economic conditions of colonial social formations, then their political specificity takes the form of an autonomous and overdeveloped state apparatus. Following recent discussions of the post-colonial state (Alavi, 1972; Saul, 1974), there are four issues which pinpoint the significance of the overdeveloped state in the post-colonial context. The original colonial administration is forced to create an extensive state apparatus in order to supervise and subordinate the indigenous social classes; the post-colonial administration inherits this overdeveloped state, especially its bureaucratic-military apparatus. The state enjoys a relatively autonomous economic role and appropriates an extensive share of the economic surplus which is then deployed 'in the name of promoting economic development' (Alavi, 1972, p. 62). Since the territories over which the post-colonial state exercises control have been typically created by administrative fiat by colonial mandates, these territorial boundaries define 'artificial entities'. The post-colonial state, therefore, is forced to create the conditions of political legitimacy and control over these territories. The state symbolises at the ideological level the unity of the social formation through the doctrine of 'national unity'. Finally, in the post-colonial context, the state is not the instrument of a single class but attempts to mediate the interests of the three dominant classes—the landlords, the small indigenous capitalist class and the comprador bourgeoisie—by securing the conditions of existence of the 'colonial mode of production', that is, by securing the conditions for the extraction of a surplus. While the state is not the direct instrument of these dominant classes, the governing class which controls the state machinery and organises the business of political administration is typically the petty bourgeoisie.

The political crises and *coups d'état* of the post-colonial social formations of the Middle East and North Africa are not to be explained by reference to essential differences between 'the West' and 'Islamic society' nor by reference to superstructural items (the doctrine of political rights). These political crises are the effects of the complex class relationships between dominant and governing classes and their struggle to control the state apparatus; these class relations are in turn the product of the specific features of the modes of production which characterise these social formations. The precise nature of these political conflicts will vary according to the particular features of each social formation. The class composition of the 'power bloc' and the structure of the political hegemony obviously show considerable variations from Morocco (Paul, 1972), Libya (First, 1974), Egypt ('Abdel-Malek, 1968), and so on. What these political regimes have in common is the central political role of the petty bourgeoisie within the state/military bureaucracy. It is the nature of this class within the total class structure of these social formations that accounts for the popularity of the ideology of a 'third way' between socialism and capitalism and the attempts to refurbish 'Islam' as a middle course. These ideologies are an expression of the ambiguity of the petty bourgeoisie which is threatened by the working class with the abolition of property and threatened with extinction by the concentration of capital (Poulantzas, 1974). Thus, the Arab petty bourgeoisie has developed an ideology based on the notion of 'non-exploiting capitalism', the communal harmony of Islam and the possibility of social development without class conflict. Nasser's 'socialism', Gadafi's 'Third Theory' and Boumedienne's 'socialism-within-Islam' are illustrations of this third way ideology (Stephens, 1971; First, 1974; Humbaraci, 1966; Kamel, n.d.). The explanation of these ideological developments is to be sought in the special features of the post-colonial state, the development of 'backward capitalism' and the ambiguities of the political role of the petty bourgeoisie. The explanation is not to be found in the 'failure' of Islam to make a step-like progression along a historical path from religion to secularism which it 'ought' to have taken.

This commentary serves to indicate a theoretical programme which would solve the No Revolutions thesis by transforming the common-sense concept of 'revolution' into a proper object of theory by reference to the theory of modes of production. This programme, however, raises a major problem in Marxist theory, namely, whether political revolutions are caused by the class struggle or whether political revolutions are effects of the transition from the dominance of one mode of production to the dominance of some other mode of production within a given social formation (Plamenatz, 1954; Shanin, 1976). My proposals for dealing with the sociology of revolutions depend upon the acceptance of certain elements of Nicos Poulantzas' theory that the presence of social classes within a social formation is to be explained in terms of overlapping modes of production and that social classes are effects of modes of production and are defined in terms of the political, ideological and economic structures (Poulantzas, 1973). There are, of course, a number of unresolved difficulties in Poulantzas' general approach to the analysis of classes and modes. While he asserts that the class struggle is crucial in explaining transformations of modes of production, the analysis of class struggle plays a secondary role to the characterisation of modes of production in his major publications (Abercrombie *et al.*, 1976). Poulantzas has attempted to deal with some of these criticisms but his various 'replies' have not changed the fundamental structure of his theory (Poulantzas, 1976). Poulantzas is forced either to abandon his original position in which 'class struggle' is subordinate to the functional requirements of the structures of the mode of production or to adhere to a voluntaristic view of class conflict (Clarke, 1977). While the contradiction between determinism and voluntarism is a significant problem, one possible answer to this difficulty in Poulantzas is to argue that 'the conditions of existence of the mode of production are secured, modified or transformed as the outcome of specific class struggles conducted under the particular conditions of the economic, political and ideological levels of the social formation' (Hindess and Hirst, 1975, p. 15). That is, the conditions which are established by the mode of production in a social formation determine the conjunctures in which the class struggle has its effects.

In this chapter, I have attempted to provide a theoretical programme for analysing the ways in which the 'colonial mode of production' establishes the conditions within which the class struggle is situated. The merits of this programme do not depend simply on the resolution of certain difficulties in Poulantzas' characterisation of the relationship between 'social classes' and 'modes of production' in the explanation of political revolutions; the programme raises the whole issue of the relationship between 'bourgeois sociology' and 'scientific Marxism'. The end of Orientalism depends not only on a critique of the historical/ philological tradition in Islamics but also on an effective critique of sociology.

Because of the tentative nature of my argument which results from the problems of developing a coherent theory of the transformation of modes of production, it could be inferred that in the last analysis Marxism has no real and effective answer to the Orientalist theme of No Revolutions in the Middle East. In order to scotch that inference, it is important to provide a conclusion which is more assertive about the positive criticisms of Orientalism which have been developed in this chapter. When Orientalists claim that what is essential to Western civilisation from classical Greece through Christianity to the present day is a set of institutions which ensured the effective possession of political rights, they abandon political analysis for political mythology. In practice, in the period of competitive capitalism, the intellectual stratum of the bourgeois class formulated the dominant *ideology* of capitalism in terms of certain juridico-political concepts relating to the imaginary rights of the private citizen. This specifically capitalist ideology cannot be regarded as the dominant political culture of slavery, feudalism and capitalism throughout European history. In feudalism, the dominant ideology is expressed through religious concepts which conceptualised society as an organic unity in which human subjects are allocated to divinely ordained places. The doctrine of 'the Great Chain of Being', the centrality of the concepts of *ordo* and *communitas*, the analogy between the functioning of the human and social body, the idea of *corpus Christi* as the sacramental key to social unity—these were the primary elements of feudal ideology. The capitalist mode in its competitive phase in which the primary requirement is the separation of the mass of labourers from the means of production is characterised by an entirely different form of dominant ideology. In capitalism where propertyless labourers are *forced* to sell their labour power because they have no alternative means of livelihood, bourgeois ideology is expressed in juridico-political concepts of a free market, free labour, equality and individual rights.

Whereas pre-capitalist social formations are characterised by notions of human subjects being bound together by 'natural' social ties (Marx and Engels, n.d., p. 52), in competitive capitalism the dominant ideology separates these human subjects from their relationships of personal inter-dependence by constituting categories of individual citizens with equality of access to the market. This ideology is a condition of existence of the legal relation of property, but it also has the important political role of attempting 'to impose upon the ensemble of society a "way of life" through which the state can be experienced as representing society's "general interest", and as the guardian of the universal vis-à-vis "private individuals"' (Poulantzas, 1973, p. 214). The effect of this ideology is to obscure the role of class interest as a force which unites 'private individuals' by presenting the nation-state as the socio-political arena within which the separate interests of privatised citizens can be recon-ciled. Bernard Lewis' argument about the centrality to the Western revolutionary tradition of the political right of resistance inflates a specific component of bourgeois political ideology under capitalism into a general empirical feature of Western societies regardless of significant differences in their economic base. Marxism, therefore, demolishes the Orientalist theory of revolutions in the West and stagnation in the East by showing it to be epistemologically idealist and ideological.

By arguing that there have been no revolutions in the Middle East, Orientalists in practice mean that there have been no 'bourgeois-democratic' revolutions in the area or, more specifically, that there are no instances of a revolutionary reorganisation of society as a result of conflicts between a traditional aristocracy and an industrial bourgeoisie where the bourgeoisie has mobilised the masses in terms of a revolution-ary theory. Since this superficial ideal typical reconstruction of capitalist history bears little relationship to the actual development of capitalism in Western societies, given that militarism, fascist ideology and the political defeat of the working class in Spain, Italy, Germany, Greece and Portugal were not exactly uncommon features of 'modernisation' (Poulantzas, 1974, 1975b), it is hardly surprising that this ideal type will not fit the political history of the Middle East. What has taken place in the Middle East is a massive transformation of pre-capitalist modes of production via the insertion of the CMP with the incorporation of these social formations into the world economy. This transformation has, however, brought about the dominance of 'backward capitalism' with its characteristic combined and unequal forms of development. The politi-cal forms of struggle within the 'power bloc' (military take-over) are determined by the structural features of the post-colonial state rather than by an Islamic preference for militarism originating in the religious concept of *jihâd*. The petty bourgeois character of the military regimes and their doctrine of Arab socialism as a Third Way are expressions at the ideological and political levels of social formations in which 'backward capitalism' intensifies and conserves the conditions of existence of archaic institutions and social structures. While the Orientalist thesis denies the genuinely oppositional character of petty bourgeois anti-colonialism, it fails to take account of the radicalising impact, despite their obvious limitations, of earlier tribal opposition to Western rule, as in the Rif Rebellion (Woolman, 1969), the Italo-Sanusi wars '(Evans-Pritchard, 1949) or the rebellion of Abd el Kader (Wolf, 1971b). These nationalist rebellions cannot be adequately subsumed under the notion of disputes between nobles any more than it is possible to dismiss political opposition in Palestine, the Arabian peninsula and Egypt (Weinstock, 1970; Chaliand, 1972; Chomsky, 1974; Halliday, 1974) as petty bourgeois fanaticism or terrorism (Avineri, 1970; Ben-Zur, 1970; Gershman, 1972).

A Marxist analysis of the revolutionary potential of political opposition, whether in the case of nineteenth century tribal rebellions or in the case of contemporary resistance, has to challenge the ethnocentric assumptions and theoretical incoherence of the dominant form of Middle East studies, namely, Orientalism. In addition, there will have to be a great deal of self-critical inspection. We have already noticed that Engels' views on Abd el Kader largely coincide with the Orientalist position that the political life of pre-colonial North Africa was merely a question of feuding and intrigue and that colonialism was essentially progressive. Furthermore, as Avineri (1976) persistently points out, Engels' observations on Oriental armies were based on the belief that 'the introduction of European military organisation with barbaric nations is far from being completed' when they have learned how to drill according to European standards. Military reform presupposed fundamental changes in the whole social structure of backward societies (Avineri, 1968a, p. 177). Such modernisation will be opposed by what Engels referred to as 'Oriental ignorance, impatience, [and] prejudice' (Avineri, 1968a, p. 177). Engels, who was affectionately known to the Marx family as 'the General' because of his knowledge of military affairs, may well have been correct in his estimation of the efficiency of the Persian army, but his opinion of 'Oriental ignorance' is not far removed from the bigotry which typified European jingoism in the nineteenth century (Kiernan, 1972). The traditional faith in the superiority of European might, which gave rise to somewhat exaggerated claims such as 'two thousand Aryans are worth a hundred thousand Chinese' during the Boxer crisis, was disturbed by 'yellow' prowess as the Russian navy disappeared below the waves at Tsushima in 1905. On a much smaller and less dramatic scale, the traditional Israeli estimation of the calibre of the Egyptian army (Avineri, 1972) was modified by the Yom Kippur War

(Laqueur, 1974). In order to demolish the Orientalist view of revolutions or to question the assumptions about the causes of military inefficiency and corruption, it will not be sufficient to call for a change of political and moral attitudes. What is required fundamentally is a demonstration of the *theoretical* inadequacy of Orientalism and its replacement by a theoretically valid alternative. While recent Marxist criticism of Orientalism has clearly achieved the work of demolition, the object of valid replacement has only been partially successful because of the theoretical difficulties which surround the analysis of social classes, ideological superstructures and modes of production.

6

Appraisal: The Dilemma of Epistemology

The controversy which constitutes this study concerns the dispute between Orientalists (historians, Arabists and Islamicists), sociologists, and Marxist political economists as to the characterisation of the history and social structure of North Africa and the Middle East. By 'Orientalism', I mean a syndrome of beliefs, attitudes and theories which infects, not only the classical works of Islamic studies, but also extensive areas of geography, economics and sociology. This syndrome consists of a number of basic arguments: (i) social development is caused by characteristics which are internal to society; (ii) the historical development of a society is either an evolutionary progress or a gradual decline; (iii) society is an 'expressive totality' in the sense that all the institutions of a society are the expression of a primary essence. These arguments allow Orientalists to establish their dichotomous ideal type of Western society whose inner essence unfolds in a dynamic progress towards democratic industrialism, and Islamic society which is either timelessly stagnant or declines from its inception. The societies of the Middle East are consequently defined by reference to a cluster of absences—the missing middle class, the missing city, the absence of political rights, the absence of revolutions. These missing features of Middle East society serve to explain why Islamic civilisation failed to produce capitalism, to generate modern personalities or to convert itself into a secular, radical culture.

My approach to the Orientalist picture of the Middle East has not been primarily to argue that their assertions turn out to be empirically false but to show the absurdity of the problems which are produced by their premises. My counterattack is based on the argument that once the global centres of capitalism had been established, the conditions for development on the periphery were fundamentally changed. The internalist theory of development fails to grasp the significance of this global relationship and consequently persists in posing futile questions about spontaneous capitalist development. The dominant character of development on the periphery is combined inequality and unevenness. Capitalism intensifies and conserves pre-capitalist modes of production so that there is no unilinear, evolutionary path from 'traditional society' to 'modern society'. On the basis of these arguments about capitalism on the periphery, all the assumptions about the universal relevance and significance of European models of development ('the bourgeois revolution', secularisation, modernisation) fall to the ground.

The critique of Orientalism, however, persistently runs into the difficulty that Marxism itself contains a heavy dosage of Orientalism, or that Marxism can be interpreted in such a manner as to make it compatible with certain aspects of Orientalism. This situation arises partly because of the overlap between Hegelian versions of Marxism and Orientalism which is illustrated by the view of history as an unfolding essence and by the specification of the static nature of 'Asiatic society'. I have chosen to illustrate this convergence by detailed reference to the work of Shlomo Avineri, not because Avineri is a straw-man who can be knocked down with a whiff of criticism, but because he offers a sophisticated Hegelian interpretation of Middle East affairs. The main problem is to undermine Avineri's Hegelian/Orientalist employment of Marx and Engels' commentaries on 'Asiatic society'. My argument has been, following Althusser (Althusser and Balibar, 1970), that there is an epistemological break in Marx's work and that Marx's journalism does not provide the basis for a scientific analysis of Asian social formations. In addition, it is possible to question the theoretical coherence of the construction of the AMP by showing that the AMP represents an arbitrary combination of relations and forces of production (Hindess and Hirst, 1975).

Having established these preliminary criticisms of the dominant assumptions of Orientalism and Hegelianism, I have attempted to demonstrate either that Marxism can demolish the whole enterprise of Orientalist speculation or that it is in principle possible to transform certain quasi-scientific problems (nationalism, the mosaic model, patrimonialism, revolutions) into proper objects of theoretical work. Again this argument is based on Althusser's view that scientific work involves breaking with ideological and quasi-scientific concepts (Generalities I) in order to create a new order of discourse (Generalities III) via the means of theoretical production (Generalities II). Unfortunately, Althusser's epistemological position is not entirely satisfactory (Fraser, 1976). This can be illustrated by asking whether there is a radical 'epistemological break' separating 'bourgeois sociology' from 'scientific Marxism' (Turner, 1977).

The critique of the Orientalist dichotomy between static traditional societies and the dynamic, industrial West, or the criticism of the Orientalist view of history as a unilinear progression towards an end-state, will not appear as a revelation to most sociologists of development. The inadequacy of ideal typical polarities is well known to sociology (Gusfield, 1967). Similarly, the assumptions about unilinear history and evolutionary progress have been effectively challenged by a variety of sociological traditions (Geertz, 1963; Wertheim, 1974). The Orientalist

view of Islam as a social cement which holds together the tattered mosaic
of Middle East societies bears a strong resemblance to the Durkheimian
view of religion as providing integrative functions for the social system.
It can hardly be said that the difficulties of postulates about the universal
functions of religious beliefs have gone unnoticed in the sociology of
religion. Furthermore, Poulantzas' view of the state as an agency which
functions to secure the conditions of existence of the dominant mode of
production, to mediate between the competing interests of classes in the
power bloc, and to give symbolic expression to the unity of the social
formation, is itself a form of sociological functionalism (Urry, 1977).
The point of these comments is not to suggest that sociology is a watered
down version of Marxism or that Marxism is sociology-plus-verbosity. It
is to recognise that as a form of discourse sociology has built into it a
self-critical tradition which is periodically institutionalised in the form of
'reflexive sociology', 'radical sociology' or 'critical sociology'
(Birnbaum, 1971; Gouldner, 1973; Bottomore, 1975; Connerton, 1976).
It is also the case that the relationship between Marxism and sociology is
not one of separation and rupture.

A further illustration can be taken from Weber's analysis of Islamic
civilisations. Weber can be criticised for providing an internalist theory
of Islamic development which concentrates on the attitudes and beliefs of
individuals as the explanation for the failure of Islamic society to
generate rational capitalism. Nevertheless Weber does produce a theory
of the political economy of Middle East societies in his account of the
prebendal features of the Islamic economy, and this theory has been
influential in subsequent analysis which purports to be Marxist
(Anderson, 1974b). It is difficult to discover any crucial difference
between Weber's view of crises in prebendalism and the central argument
of recent attempts to use the AMP to describe the Ottoman system
(Keyder, 1976; Islamoğlu and Keyder, 1977). What Keyder adds to
Weber's prebendalism is a discussion of the role of merchant capital in
social formations which are being forced to the periphery of the capitalist world. However, his arguments about the world-system are taken
from Wallerstein (1974) who also draws on Weber's sociology. What I
am claiming here is that the information (or 'knowledges') which
Marxists pump into their theoretical work at the point of Generalities I is
typically dependent on sociological research and that the processes
(Generalities II) by which this information is transformed are far from
clear. This problem is present in Hindess and Hirst (1975) when they
reproduce an anthropological problematic in L. H. Morgan's distinction
between *societas/civitas* in their primitive communist mode of production (Asad and Wolpe, 1976).

Finally, it is important to bear in mind the complex relationship
between Marxism and sociology over the problems of determinism and
voluntarism. While Weberian sociology tends towards a position of

causal indeterminacy in which various institutional orders (politics, religion, law, economy) are inter-correlated with each other, traditional Marxism has been committed to notions about material causality. In traditional Marxism, either the economic base is the cause of events that take place in the superstructure of law and politics or the struggle between social classes is the causal agent. Most 'structuralist Marxists', especially Poulantzas, have been concerned to reject economism and the implication that everything in the social formation can be read off from the base. By a variety of theoretical devices—the relative autonomy of the state from the economy, the separation of ideology, politics and economics—Poulantzas has attempted to break with simple economic determinism. However, since the determination of the social formation by the mode of production in dominance plays the central role in Poulantzas' understanding of capitalism, it has been claimed that he fails to recognise the significance of class struggle and consequently ends with a 'structural super-determinism' (Miliband, 1970). Because certain features of Althusserian-Poulantzasian structuralism played a major part in formulating the basic approach of *Pre-Capitalist Modes of Production*, Hindess and Hirst (1977) came eventually to reject many of their previous assumptions. Their auto-critique abandons the distinction between social formations and modes of production, rejects the concept of mode of production and the whole epistemological basis of their previous work. Two crucial features of the new theory are (i) that 'political forces and ideological forms cannot be reduced to the expressions of "interests" determined at the level of economic class relations' (Hindess and Hirst, 1977, p. 57), and (ii) that 'there can be no "knowledge" in political practice' (Hindess and Hirst, 1977, p. 59) since politics involves the calculation of the effects of possible courses of action and no general, deterministic theory can be a guide to the analysis of concrete political situations. Just as Zubaida (1977) argued that there can be no general theory or definition of 'nationalism', so apparently Hindess and Hirst want to claim that political facts cannot be objects of Marxist theory because political action and calculation are somehow pre-theoretical or a-theoretical. Their attempt to put the 'class struggle' back in the picture, their separation of politics from theory and their rejection of economic causality have at least one odd consequence which leads one to the view that their auto-critique is a retrograde step. While some of their arguments are buttressed by references to Lenin's views on the analysis of the 'current situation', the consequence is to achieve a profound shift of their position toward Weberian sociology. Since Weber also believes that general theory can be of no avail in matters of political calculation, and that politics and culture cannot be reduced to economic class relations, it is difficult to see how Marxism could ever be distinguished from sociology on these grounds.

These highly critical comments on Hindess and Hirst are motivated by the belief that *Pre-Capitalist Modes of Production* is a profound contribution to the whole issue of rethinking problems in Marxist theory, in particular of the relationship between the analysis of modes of production and class analysis. Marxism operates at two *theoretical* levels which involve the analysis of the mode of production and the necessary conditions of existence which guarantee the reproduction of that mode at a formal level. At the next theoretical level, Marxist analysis focuses on conjunctures in the social formation, namely, the relationships between dominant and subordinate modes, their conditions of existence and the struggle between social classes over the appropriation of an economic surplus. At this level, while the mode of production determines the general conditions of the class struggle, the conflict between social classes has direct effects on the principal contradictions of the mode, its laws of motion and reproduction. There is no warrant for believing that certain phenomena are pre-theoretical or that Marxism could abandon some adherence to the laws of economic determination, however complex or 'superstructural', or that the concept of the 'mode of production' could be easily discarded.

The criticism of Orientalism in its various forms requires something more than the valid but indecisive notion that at its worst Orientalist scholarship was a rather thin disguise for attitudes of moral or racial superiority (Asad, 1973) and thereby a justification for colonialism. What is needed is something other than the objection that some Orientalists were less than neutral and objective, or that they retired from the real world of Middle East politics to the ivory tower of philology, poetry and aesthetics. The end of Orientalism requires a fundamental attack on the theoretical and epistemological roots of Orientalist scholarship which creates the long tradition of Oriental Despotism, mosaic societies and the 'Muslim City'. Modern Marxism is fully equipped to do this work of destruction, but in this very activity Marxism displays its own internal theoretical problems and uncovers those analytical cords which tie it to Hegelianism, to nineteenth-century political economy and to Weberian sociology. The end of Orientalism, therefore, also requires the end of certain forms of Marxist thought and the creation of a new type of analysis.

References

Abdel-Malek, Anouar, 'Nasserism and socialism', *Socialist Register* (1964), pp. 38-55.

Abdel-Malek, Anouar, *Egypt, A Military Society* (New York, Random House, 1968).

Abercrombie, N., Turner, B. S. and Urry, J. 'Class, state and fascism: the work of Nicos Poulantzas', *Political Studies*, vol. 24 (1976), pp. 510-19.

Abou-Zeid, Ahmed M., 'The changing world of the nomads', in Peristiany, 1968, pp. 279-88.

Abrahamian, Ervand, 'Oriental despotism: the case of Qajar Iran', *International Journal of Middle East Studies*, vol. 5 (1974), pp. 3-31.

Abrahamian, Ervand, 'European feudalism and Middle Eastern despotism', *Science and Society*, vol. 39 (1975), pp. 129-56.

Abun-Nasr, J., 'The Salafiyya movement in Morocco: the religious bases of the Moroccan nationalist movement', *St. Antony's Papers*, vol. 16 (1963), pp. 90-105.

Alavi, Hamza, 'The state in post-colonial societies—Pakistan and Bangladesh', *New Left Review*, no. 74 (1972), pp. 59-81.

Al-Azmeh, Aziz, 'What is the Islamic city?', *Review of Middle East Studies*, vol. 2 (1976), pp. 1-12.

al-Qazzaz, Ayad, 'Sociology in underdeveloped countries', *The Sociological Review*, vol. 20 (1972), pp. 93-103.

Althusser, Louis, *For Marx* (Harmondsworth, Penguin Books, 1969).

Althusser, Louis, *Lenin and Philosophy and Other Essays* (London, New Left Books, 1971).

Althusser, Louis and Balibar, Etienne, *Reading Capital* (London, New Left Books, 1970).

Amin, Samir, *The Maghreb and the Modern World* (Harmondsworth, Penguin Books, 1970).

Anderson, Perry, 'Origins of the present crisis', *New Left Review*, no. 23 (1964), pp. 26-54.

Anderson, Perry, *Passages from Antiquity to Feudalism* (London, New Left Books, 1974a).

Anderson, Perry, *Lineages of the Absolutist State* (London, New Left Books, 1974b).

Antonius, George, *The Arab Awakening* (London, 1938).

Antoun, Richard T., 'Anthropology', in Binder, 1976, pp. 137-99.

Apter, David E., *The Politics of Modernization* (Chicago, University of Chicago Press, 1965).

Arab League Office, *Israeli Socialism: a reality or a myth?* (London, n.d.).

Arkadie, Brian van, 'The impact of the Israeli occupation on the economics of the West Bank and Gaza', *Journal of Palestine Studies*, vol. 6 (1977), pp. 103-29.

Aruri, Naseer (ed.), *The Palestinian Resistance to Israeli Occupation* (Wilmette, Illinois, The Medina University Press International, 1970).

Asad, Talal (ed.), *Anthropology and the Colonial Encounter* (London, Ithaca Press, 1973).

Asad, Talal, 'The rise of Arab nationalism: a comment', in Davis *et al.*, 1975, pp. 93-6.

Asad, Talal, 'Politics and religion in Islamic reform: a critique of Kedourie's *Afghani and Abduh*', *Review of Middle East Studies*, no. 2 (1976), pp. 13-22.

Asad, Talal and Wolpe, Harold, 'Concepts of modes of production', *Economy and Society*, vol. 5 (1976), pp. 470-505.

Aulas, Marie-Christine, 'Sadat's Egypt', *New Left Review*, no. 98 (1976), pp. 84-97.

Avineri, Shlomo, 'Hegel and nationalism', *Review of Politics*, vol. 24 (1962), pp. 461-84.

Avineri, Shlomo, 'The Hegelian origins of Marx's political thought', *Review of Metaphysics*, vol. 21 (1967), pp. 33-50.

Avineri, Shlomo (ed.), *Karl Marx on Colonialism and Modernization* (New York, Garden City, Doubleday, 1968a).

Avineri, Shlomo, *The Social and Political Thought of Karl Marx* (London, Cambridge University Press, 1968b).

Avineri, Shlomo, 'The Palestinians and Israel', *Commentary*, vol. 49 (1970), pp. 31-44.

Avineri, Shlomo (ed.), *Israel and the Palestinians* (New York, St Martins Press, 1971).

Avineri, Shlomo, 'Modernization and Arab society: some reflections', in Howe and Gershman, 1972, pp. 300-11.

Avineri, Shlomo, 'Political and social aspects of Israeli and Arab nationalism', in Kamenka, 1976, pp. 101-22.

Ayyash, Abdul-Ilah Abu, 'Israeli regional planning policy in the occupied Arab territories', *Journal of Palestine Studies*, vol. 5 (1976), pp. 83-108.

Baer, Gabriel, *Population and Society in the Arab East* (London, Routledge & Kegan Paul, 1964).

Banaji, Jairus, 'For a theory of colonial modes of production', *Economic and Political Weekly*, vol. 7 (1972), pp. 2498-502.

Banaji, Jairus, 'Backward capitalism, primitive accumulation and modes of production', *Journal of Contemporary Asia*, vol. 3 (1973), pp. 393-413.

Banaji, Jairus, 'Modes of production in a materialist conception of history' (n.d., mimeo).

Baran, Paul A., *The Political Economy of Growth* (Harmondsworth, Penguin Books, 1973).

Barratt Brown, M., *The Economics of Imperialism* (Harmondsworth, Penguin Books, 1974).

Barth, F., *Nomads of South Persia* (Oslo, Universitetsforlaget, 1964).

Bellah, Robert N., 'Reflections on the Protestant ethic analogy in Asia', *Journal of Social Issues*, vol. 29 (1963), pp. 52-60.

Ben-Porath, Y., *The Arab Labour Force in Israel* (Jerusalem, Israel Universities Press, 1966).

Ben-Zur, A., 'The social composition of the Ba'ath party membership in the Kuneitra district', in Goldberg, 1970, pp. 235-43.

Berger, M., *Bureaucracy and Society in Modern Egypt* (Princeton, Princeton University Press, 1957).

Berger, M., *The Arab World Today* (Garden City, New York, Anchor Books, 1964).

Berkes, Niyazi (ed.), *Turkish Nationalism and Western Civilization: Selected Essays of Ziya Gökalp* (London, Allen & Unwin, 1959).

Berger, M., *The Development of Secularism in Turkey* (Montreal, McGill University Press, 1964).

Berki, R. N., 'On Marxian thought and the problem of international relations', *World Politics*, vol. 24 (1971), pp. 80-105.

Berlin, Isaiah, 'The life and opinions of Moses Hess', in Rieff, 1970, pp. 137-82.

Bhagwati, J. (ed.), *Economics and World Order from the 1970s to the 1990s* (London, Collier-Macmillan, 1972).

Bill, James A., 'Class analysis and the dialectics of modernization in the Middle East', *International Journal of Middle East Studies*, vol. 3 (1972), pp. 417-34.

Binder, Leonard, *Politics in the Lebanon* (New York, Wiley, 1966).

Binder, Leonard (ed.), *The Study of the Middle East* (New York, Wiley, 1976).

Birnbaum, Norman, *Toward a Critical Sociology* (London, Oxford University Press, 1971).

Bloom, Soloman F., 'Karl Marx and the Jews', *Jewish Social Studies*, vol. 4 (1942), pp. 3-16.

Bober, Arie (ed.), *The Other Israel: the radical case against Zionism* (Garden City, New York, Doubleday, 1972).

Bocock, Robert J., 'The Ismailis in Tanzania: a Weberian analysis', *British Journal of Sociology*, vol. 22 (1971), pp. 365-80.

Borochov, Ber, *Nationalism and the Class Struggle: a Marxian approach to the Jewish problem* (New York, 1937).

Bottomore, T. B., *Sociology as Social Criticism* (London, Allen & Unwin, 1975).

Braverman, H., *Labor and Monopoly Capital* (New York and London, Monthly Review Press, 1974).

Brinton, Crane, *The Anatomy of Revolution* (New York, Vintage Books, 1965).

Bukharin, N., *Imperialism and World Economy* (London, Merlin Press, 1972).

Bullock, P. and Yaffe, D., 'Inflation, the crisis and the post-war boom', *Revolutionary Communist*, no. 3 (1975), pp. 5-45.

Burke, Edmund, 'Morocco and the Near East: reflections on some basic differences', *Archives européennes de sociologie*, vol. 10 (1969), pp. 70-94.

Burke, Edmund, 'The image of the Moroccan state in French ethnological literature: a new look at the origin of Lyautey's Berber policy', in Gellner and Micaud, 1973, pp. 175-199.

Burrow, J. W., *Evolution and Society: a study in Victorian social theory* (London, Cambridge University Press, 1970).

Carlebach, Julius, *Karl Marx and the Radical Critique of Judaism* (London, Routledge & Kegan Paul, 1977).

CERM, *Sur le 'Mode de Production Asiatique'* (Paris, 1969).

Chaliand, Gérard, *The Palestinian Resistance* (Harmondsworth, Penguin Books, 1972).

Charvet, John, *The Social Problem in the Philosophy of Rousseau* (London, Cambridge University Press, 1974).

Chomsky, Noam, *Peace in the Middle East?* (London, Fontana/Collins, 1974).

Clammer, John (ed.), *The New Economic Anthropology* (London, Macmillan, forthcoming).

Clarke, Simon, 'Marxism, sociology and Poulantzas' theory of the state', *Capital and Class*, no. 2 (1977), pp. 1-31.

Connerton, Paul (ed.), *Critical Sociology* (Harmondsworth, Penguin Books, 1976).

Cooley, John K., *Green March, Black September* (London, Frank Cass, 1973).

Coon, Carleton S., *Caravan: the story of the Middle East* (New York, Holt, Rinehart & Winston, 1951).

Coury, Ralph, 'Why can't they be like us?', *Review of Middle East Studies*, no. 1 (1975), p. 113-33.

Davies, James C., 'Toward a theory of revolution', *American Sociological Review*, vol. 27 (1962), pp. 5-19.

Davis, H. B., 'Nations, colonies and classes: the position of Marx and Engels', *Science and Society*, vol. 29 (1965), pp. 26-43.

Davis, Uri, *Israel: Utopia Incorporated* (London, Zed Press, 1977).

Davis, Uri, Mack, A. and Yuval-Davis, N. (eds.), *Israel and the Palestinians* (London, Ithaca Press, 1975).

Dekmejian, R. Hrair, *Egypt under Nasser* (Albany, State University of New York Press, 1971).

Dodwell, H. H., *The Founder of Modern Egypt: a study of Muhammad Ali* (London, Cambridge University Press, 1967).

Dos Santos, T., 'The structure of dependence', *American Economic Review*, vol. 60 (1970), pp. 231-6.

Dunn, J., *Modern Revolutions: an introduction to the analysis of a political phenomenon* (London, Cambridge University Press, 1972).

Duvignaud, Jean, 'Pratique de la sociologie dans les pays décolonisés', *Cahiers internationaux de sociologie*, vol. 34 (1963), pp. 165-74.

Duvignaud, Jean, 'Classes et conscience de classe dans un pays du Maghreb: la Tunisie', *Cahiers internationaux de sociologie*, vol. 38 (1965), pp. 185-200.

Easton, Loyd D. and Guddat, Kurt H. (eds.), *Writings of the Young Marx on Philosophy and Society* (Garden City, New York, Anchor Books, 1967).

Eckstein, Harry, 'On the etiology of internal wars', *History and Theory*, vol. 4 (1965), pp. 133-63.

Edens, David G., 'The anatomy of the Saudi revolution', *International Journal of Middle East Studies*, vol. 5 (1974), pp. 50-64.

Emmanuel, A., 'White settler colonialism and the myth of investment imperialism', *New Left Review*, no. 73 (1972), pp. 35-57.

Engels, F., *The Condition of the Working Class in England in 1844* (London, Allen & Unwin, 1968).

Evans-Pritchard, E. E., *The Sanusi of Cyrenaica* (London, Oxford University Press, 1949).

Farsoun, Karen, 'State capitalism in Algeria', *MERIP Reports*, no. 35 (1975), pp. 3-30.

Farsoun, K., Farsoun, S. and Ajay, A., 'Mid-East perspectives from the American left', *Journal of Palestine Studies*, vol. 4 (1974), pp. 94-119.

Fernbach, D. (ed.), *Surveys from Exile* (Harmondsworth, Penguin Books, 1973).

Feuer, Lewis S. (ed.), *Marx and Engels: Basic Writings on Politics and Philosophy* (London, Fontana Books, 1971).

First, Ruth, *Libya: the elusive revolution* (Harmondsworth, Penguin Books, 1974).

Fisher, S. N. (ed.), *Social Forces in the Middle East* (New York, Ithaca, 1955).

Foster-Carter, A., 'Neo-marxist approaches to development and underdevelopment', in Kadt and Williams, 1974, pp. 67-105.

Frank, A. G., *Capitalism and Underdevelopment in Latin America* (New York, Monthly Review Press, 1969).

Fraser, John, 'Louis Althusser on science, Marxism and politics', *Science and Society*, vol. 40 (1976), pp. 438-64.

Gallissot, René, 'Precolonial Algeria', *Economy and Society*, vol. 4 (1975), pp. 418-45.

Geertz, Clifford, *The Religion of Java* (New York, Free Press, 1960).

Geertz, Clifford, *Agricultural Involution: the process of ecological change in Indonesia* (California, California University Press, 1963).

Gellner, Ernest, 'Sanctity, puritanism, secularisation and nationalism in North Africa', *Archives de sociologie des religions*, vol. 8 (1963), pp. 71-86.

Gellner, Ernest, *Thought and Change* (London, Weidenfeld & Nicolson, 1964).

Gellner, Ernest, *Saints of the Atlas* (London, Weidenfeld & Nicolson, 1969).

Gellner, Ernest, 'Patterns of tribal rebellion in Morocco', in Vatikiotis, 1972, pp. 120-45.

Gellner, Ernest and Micaud, Charles (eds.), *Arabs and Berbers: from tribe to nation* (London, Duckworth, 1973).

George, A.R., 'Forgotten Arabs of Israel', *Middle East International*, no. 21 (1973), pp. 16-18.

Geras, Norman, 'Essence and appearance: aspects of fetishism in Marx's *Capital*', *New Left Review*, no. 65 (1971), pp. 68-86.

Gerassi, John (ed.), *Towards Revolution*, vol. 1 (London, Weidenfeld & Nicolson, 1971).

Gershman, Carl, 'The failure of the fedayeen', in Howe and Gershman, 1972, pp. 224-48.

Ghilan, Maxim, *How Israel Lost its Soul* (Harmondsworth, Penguin Books, 1974).

Gibb, H. A. R. and Bowen, H., *Islamic Society and the West: a study of the impact of Western civilisation on Moslem culture in the Near East* (London, Oxford University Press, 1950 and 1957), 2 vols.

Giddens, Anthony, *Politics and Sociology in the Thought of Max Weber* (London, Macmillan, 1972).

Giddens, Anthony, *The Class Structure of the Advanced Societies* (London, Hutchinson, 1973).

Glass, Charles, 'Jews against Zionism: Israeli Jewish anti-Zionism', *Journal of Palestine Studies*, vol. 5 (1976), pp. 56-81.

Goitein, S. D., 'The rise of the near-eastern bourgeoisie in early Islamic times', *Journal of World History*, vol. 3 (1957), pp. 583-604.

Goldberg, Zeev (ed.), *Arab Socialism* (Beit Berl, 1970), in Hebrew.

Goldmann, L., *The Philosophy of the Enlightenment* (London, Routledge & Kegan Paul, 1973).

Goodridge, Martin, 'The ages of faith: romance or reality?', *The Sociological Review*, vol. 23 (1975), pp. 381-96.

Gordon, L. A. and Fridman, L. A., 'Peculiarities in the composition and structure of the working class in the economically underdeveloped countries of Asia and Africa (the example of India and the UAR)', in Thornton, 1964, pp. 154-88.

Gouldner, Alvin W., *For Sociology: renewal and critique in sociology today* (Harmondsworth, Penguin Books, 1973).

Gusfield, Joseph, 'Tradition and modernity: misplaced polarities in the study of social change', *American Journal of Sociology*, vol. 72 (1967), pp. 351-62.

Haddad, Robert M., *Syrian Christians in Muslim Society* (Princeton, Princeton University Press, 1970).

Hagopian, Edward and Zahlan, A. B., 'Palestine's Arab population: the demography of the Palestinians', *Journal of Palestine Studies*, vol. 3 (1974), pp. 32-73.

Halliday, Fred, *Arabia without Sultans* (Harmondsworth, Penguin Books, 1974).

Halpern, M., 'Middle Eastern armies and the new middle class', in Johnson, 1962, pp. 277-315.

Halpern, M., 'Egypt and the new middle class: reaffirmations and new explorations', *Comparative Studies in Society and History*, vol. 11 (1969), pp. 97-108.

Hanoteau, Adolphe and Letourneux, Ernest, *La Kabylie et les coutumes kabyles* (Paris, Augustin Challamel, 1893).

Harari, Yahiel, *The Arabs in Israel: Facts and Figures* (Givat Haviva, Center for Arab and Afro-Asian Studies, 1974).

Hegel, G. W. F., *The Philosophy of History* (New York, Dover Publications, 1956).

Hilal, Jamil, 'Class transformation in the West Bank and Gaza', *MERIP Reports*, no. 53 (1976), pp. 9-15.

Hill, Michael (ed.), *A Sociological Yearbook of Religion in Britain* (London, SCM, 1975).

Hindess, Barry and Hirst, Paul Q., *Pre-Capitalist Modes of Production* (London and Boston, Routledge & Kegan Paul, 1975).

Hindess, Barry and Hirst, Paul Q., *Mode of Production and Social Formation: an auto-critique of Pre-Capitalist Modes of Production* (London, Macmillan, 1977).

Hirst, Paul Q., 'Problems and advances in the theory of ideology' (mimeo, 1976).

Hobsbawm, Eric, Introduction to K. Marx, *Pre-Capitalist Economic Formations* (New York, International Publishers, 1965).

Hodgson, Marshall G. S., *The Venture of Islam* (Chicago and London, University of Chicago Press, 1974), 3 vols.

Holt, P. M., *Egypt and the Fertile Crescent 1516-1922* (London, Longmans, 1966).

Hone, Angus, 'The primary commodities boom', *New Left Review*, no. 81 (1973), pp. 82-92.

Hoselitz, Bert F. and Moore, Wilbert E. (eds), *Industrialization and Society* (UNESCO, Mouton, 1963).

Hourani, A. H. *Syria and Lebanon* (London, Oxford University Press, 1946).

Hourani, A. H., *Minorities in the Arab World* (London, Oxford University Press, 1947).

Hourani, A. H., 'Ottoman reform and the politics of notables', in Polk and Chambers, 1968, pp. 41-68.

Hourani, A. H., 'Revolutions in the Middle East', in Vatikiotis, 1972, pp. 65-72.

Howe, Irving and Gershman, Carl (eds.), *Israel, the Arabs and the Middle East* (New York, Bantam Books, 1972).

Humbaraci, Arslan, *Algeria: a revolution that failed* (London, Pall Mall Press, 1966).

Hussein, Mahmoud, *Class Conflict in Egypt: 1945-1970* (New York, Monthly Review Press, 1973).

Hymer, S., 'The multinational corporation and the law of uneven development', in Bhagwati, 1972, pp. 113-40.

Inalcik, H., 'Bursa and the commerce of the Levant', *Journal of Economic and Social History of the Orient*, vol. 3 (1960), pp. 131-47.

Inalcik, H., 'Capital formation in the Ottoman empire', *Journal of Economic History*, vol. 29 (1969), pp. 97-140.

Inkeles, A. and Smith, David H., *Becoming Modern* (London, Heinemann Educational Books, 1974).

Islamoğlu, H. and Keyder, C., 'Agenda for Ottoman history' (mimeo, 1977).

Issawi, Charles, *Egypt in Revolution: an economic analysis* (London, Oxford University Press, 1963).

Issawi, Charles (ed.), *The Economic History of the Middle East 1800-1914* (Chicago and London, Chicago University Press, 1966).

Jaafari, Lafi, 'The brain drain to the United States: the migration of Jordanian and Palestinian professionals and students', *Journal of Palestine Studies*, vol. 3 (1973), pp. 119-31.

Jankowski, James P., 'The Palestinian Arab revolt of 1936-1939', *The Muslim World*, vol. 63 (1973), pp. 220-33.

Janowitz, M., *The Military in the Political Development of New Nations* (Chicago, University of Chicago Press, 1964).

Jiryis, Sabri, 'The legal structure for the expropriation and absorption of Arab lands in Israel', *Journal of Palestine Studies*, vol. 2 (1973), pp. 82-104.

Jiryis, Sabri, *The Arabs in Israel* (New York, Monthly Review Press, 1976).

Johnson, J. J. (ed.), *The Role of the Military in Underdeveloped Countries* (Princeton, Princeton University Press, 1962).

Johnson, M., 'Confessionalism and individualism in Lebanon', *Review of Middle East Studies*, no. 1 (1975), pp. 79-91.

Jones, M., 'Israel, Palestine and socialism', *Socialist Register* (1970), pp. 63-87.

Kadt, Emanuel de and Williams, Gavin (eds.), *Sociology and Development* (London, Tavistock, 1974).

Kamel, Michel, 'Political and ideological role of the petit-bourgeoisie in the Arab world' (mimeo, n.d.).

Kamenka, E. (ed.), *Nationalism: the nature and evolution of an idea* (London, Arnold, 1976).

Kay, Geoffrey, *Development and Underdevelopment: a marxist analysis* (London, Macmillan, 1975).

Keddie, Nikki R., *An Islamic Response to Imperialism* (Berkeley and Los Angeles, University of California Press, 1968).

Kedourie, Elie, *Nationalism* (London, Hutchinson, 1960).

Kedourie, Elie, 'Further light on Afghani', *Middle Eastern Studies*, no. 1 (1965), pp. 187-202.

Kedourie, Elie, *Afghani and Abduh: an essay on religious unbelief and political activism in modern Islam* (London, Cass, 1966).

Kedourie, Elie (ed.), *Nationalism in Asia and Africa* (London, Weidenfeld & Nicolson, 1970).

Kelidar, Abbas, 'The rise of Arab nationalism', in Davis *et al.*, 1975, pp. 80-93.

Keyder, Caglar, 'The dissolution of the Asiatic mode of production', *Economy and Society*, vol. 5 (1976), pp. 178-96.

Khadduri, M., 'The role of the military in the Middle East politics', *American Political Science Review*, vol. 46 (1953), pp. 511-24.

Khadduri, M., 'The army officer: his role in Middle Eastern politics', in Fisher, 1955, pp. 162-84.

Kiernan, V. G., *The Lords of Human Kind* (Harmondsworth, Penguin Books, 1972).

Kodsy, Ahmed El and Lobel, Eli, *The Arab World and Israel* (New York and London, Monthly Review Press, 1970).

Koebner, R., 'Despot and despotism: vicissitudes of a political term', *Journal of the Warburg and Courtauld Institutes*, vol. 14 (1951), pp. 275-302.

Kolakowski, Leszek, 'Marxist philosophy and national reality: natural communities and universal brotherhood', *Round Table*, no. 253 (1974), pp. 43-55.

Kramnick, Isaac, 'Reflections on revolution: definition and explanation in recent scholarship', *History and Theory*, vol. 11 (1972), pp. 26-63.

Lapidus, Ira M., 'Muslim cities and Islamic societies', in Lapidus, 1969, pp. 47-79 (1969a).

Lapidus, Ira M. (ed.), *Middle East Cities* (Berkeley and Los Angeles, University of California Press, 1969) (1969b).

Laqueur, Walter, *Confrontation: the Middle East War and World Politics* (London, Abacus, 1974).

Langer, Felicia, *With My Own Eyes* (London, Ithaca Press, 1975).

Laroui, Abdallah, 'For a methodology of Islamic studies', *Diogenes*, no. 83 (1973), pp. 12-39.

Lenin, V. I., 'Imperialism, the highest stage of capitalism', in *Essential Works of Lenin* (New York, Bantam Books, 1971).

Lerner, Daniel, *The Passing of Traditional Society* (New York, Free Press, 1958).

Lewis, Bernard, *The Emergence of Modern Turkey* (London, Oxford University Press, 1961).

Lewis, Bernard, *The Arabs in History* (London, Hutchinson University Library, 1964).

Lewis, Bernard, 'The impact of the French revolution on Turkey', in Métraux and Crouzet, 1965, pp. 31-59.

Lewis, Bernard, 'Islamic concepts of revolution', in Vatikiotis, 1972, pp. 30-40.

Lichtheim, George, 'Marx and the "Asiatic mode of production"', *St. Antony's Papers*, no. 14 (1963), pp. 86-112.

Lichtheim, George, *A Short History of Socialism* (London, Weidenfeld & Nicolson, 1970).

Lichtman, Richard, 'The facade of equality in liberal democratic theory', *Socialist Revolution*, vol. 1 (1970), pp. 85-125.

Lukács, Georg, *History and Class Consciousness* (London, Merlin Press, 1971).

McClelland, David, *The Achieving Society* (New York, van Nostrand, 1961).

McClelland, David, 'National character and economic growth in Turkey and Iran', in Pye, 1963, pp. 152-81 (1963a).

McClelland, David, 'The achievement motive in economic growth', in Hoselitz and Moore, 1963, pp. 74-96 (1963b).

McLellan, David, *Karl Marx: His Life and Thought* (London, Macmillan, 1973).

Makarius, R., *La jeunesse intellectualle d'Egypte au lendemain de la deuxième guerre mondiale* (La Haye, Mouton, 1960).

Mann, Michael, *Consciousness and Action among the Western Working Class* (London, Macmillan, 1973).

Mansfield, Peter, *Nasser's Egypt* (Harmondsworth, Penguin Books, 1969).

Mardin, S., 'Power, civil society and culture in the Ottoman empire', *Comparative Studies in Society and History*, vol. 11 (1969), pp. 258-81.

Marx, Karl, *Capital* (London, Lawrence & Wishart, 1970), 3 vols.

Marx, Karl, *A Contribution to the Critique of Political Economy* (London, Lawrence & Wishart, 1971).

Marx, Karl, 'The eighteenth Brumaire of Louis Bonaparte', in Fernbach, 1973, pp. 143-249.

Marx, Karl and Engels, F., *The Communist Manifesto* (Moscow, Foreign Publishing House, n.d.).

Marx, Karl and Engels, F., *On Ireland* (London, Lawrence & Wishart, 1968).

Marx, Karl and Engels, F., *On Colonialism* (New York, International Publishers, 1972).

Marx, Karl and Engels, F., *The German Ideology* (London, Lawrence & Wishart, 1974).

Melotti, Umberto, *Marx and the Third World* (London, Macmillan, 1977).

Mepham, John, 'The theory of ideology in *Capital*', *Radical Philosophy*, no. 2 (1972), pp. 12-19.

Mészáros, I., *Marx's Theory of Alienation* (London, Merlin Press, 1970).

Métraux, Guy and Crouzet, François (eds), *The New Asia* (New York, UNESCO, Mentor Books, 1965).

Meyer, G., 'Early German socialism and Jewish emancipation', *Jewish Social Studies*, vol. 1 (1939), pp. 409-22.

Miliband, Ralph, 'The capitalist state: a reply to Nicos Poulantzas', *New Left Review*, no. 59 (1970), pp. 53-60.

Minogue, K. R., *Nationalism* (London, Batsford, 1967).

Mitchell, M. Marion, 'Emile Durkheim and the philosophy of nationalism', *Political Science Quarterly*, vol. 46 (1931), pp. 87-106.

Moore Jr, Barrington, *Social Origins of Dictatorship and Democracy* (Boston, Beacon Press, 1966).

Muhsam, H. V., 'Sedentarization of the Bedouin in Israel', *International Social Science Bulletin*, vol. 11 (1959), pp. 539-49.

Murray, Roger and Wengraf, Tom, 'The Algerian revolution', *New Left Review*, no. 22 (1963), pp. 14-65.

Nahas, Dunia, *The Israeli Communist Party* (London, Ithaca Press, 1976).

Nairn, Tom, 'Marxism and the modern Janus', *New Left Review*, no. 94 (1975), pp. 3-29.

Nurkse, R., *Problems of Capital Formation in Underdeveloped Countries* (London, Oxford University Press, 1953).

Outhwaite, W., *Understanding Social Life* (London, Allen & Unwin, 1975).

Owen, E. R. J., *Cotton and the Egyptian Economy 1820-1914: a study in trade and development* (London, Oxford University Press, 1969).

Owen, E. R. J. (ed.), *Essays on the Crisis in Lebanon* (London, Ithaca Press, 1976).

Parkin, F., *Class Inequality and Political Order* (London, Paladin, 1972).

Patai, R., 'Nomadism: Middle Eastern and central Asian', *Southwestern Journal of Anthropology*, vol. 7 (1951), pp. 401-14.

Pateman, Trevor (ed.), *Counter Course* (Harmondsworth, Penguin Books, 1972).

Paul, James A., 'The Moroccan crisis: nationalism and imperialism on Europe's periphery', *Monthly Review*, October (1972), pp. 15-43.

Peel, J. D. Y., 'Cultural factors in the contemporary theory of development', *Archives européennes de sociologie*, vol. 14 (1973), pp. 283-303.

Peristiany, J. G. (ed.), *Contributions to Mediterranean Sociology* (Paris, Mouton, 1968).

Perlmutter, Amos, 'Egypt and the myth of the new middle class: a comparative analysis', *Comparative Studies in Society and History*, vol. 10 (1967), pp. 46-65.

Perlmutter, Amos, 'The myth of the myth of the new middle class: some lessons in social and political theory', *Comparative Studies in Society and History*, vol. 12 (1970), pp. 14-26.

Peters, Emrys L., 'The tied and the free', in Peristiany, 1968, pp. 167-88.

Plamenatz, John, *German Marxism and Russian Communism* (London, Longmans, 1954).

Plant, Raymond, *Hegel* (London, Allen & Unwin, 1973).

Polk, W. R. and Chambers, R. C. (eds), *The Beginnings of Modernization in the Middle East* (Chicago, 1968).

Poulantzas, Nicos, *Political Power and Social Classes* (London, New Left Books and Sheed & Ward, 1973).

Poulantzas, Nicos, *Fascism and Dictatorship* (London, New Left Books, 1974).

Poulantzas, Nicos, *Classes in Contemporary Capitalism* (London, New Left Books, 1975a).

Poulantzas, Nicos, *La Crise des dictatures: Portugal, Grèce, Espagne* (Paris, Maspero, 1975b).

Poulantzas, Nicos, 'The capitalist state: a reply to Miliband and Laclau', *New Left Review*, no. 95 (1976), pp. 63-83.

Pye, Lucian W. (ed.), *Communications and Political Development* (Princeton, Princeton University Press, 1963).

Radwan, Samir, *Capital Formation in Egyptian Industry and Agriculture 1882-1967* (London, Ithaca Press, 1974).

Renan, E., *Discours et conférences* (Paris, 1887).

Rieff, Philip (ed.), *On Intellectuals* (Garden City, New York, Anchor Books, Doubleday, 1970).

Rodinson, Maxime, *Islam et capitalisme* (Paris, Seuil, 1966; English translation, Allen Lane, 1974).

Rodinson, Maxime, *Israel: a Colonial-Settler State?* (New York, Monad Press, 1973).

Rostow, W. W., *Stages of Economic Growth* (London, Cambridge University Press, 1960).

Rustow, D., 'The army and the founding of the Turkish Republic', *World Politics*, vol. 11 (1959), pp. 513-52.

Ryan, Sheila, 'The Israeli economic policy in the occupied areas: foundations of a new imperialism', *MERIP Reports*, no. 24 (1974), pp. 7-8.

Saba, Paul, 'The creation of the Lebanese economy', in Owen, 1976, pp. 1-22.

Salem, Elie, 'Arab reformers and the reinterpretation of Islam', *Muslim World*, vol. 55 (1965), pp. 311-20.

Saul, John S., 'The state in post-colonial societies: Tanzania', *The Socialist Register* (1974), pp. 349-72.

Seddon, David, 'Economic anthropology or political economy?', in Clammer, forthcoming.

Shaicovitch, B., 'Dialectical materialism: Marx and the West Bank', *New Middle East*, no. 55 (1973), pp. 21-5.

Shanin, Teodor, 'The third stage: Marxist social theory and the origins of our time', *Journal of Contemporary Asia*, vol. 6 (1976), pp. 289-308.

Shanin, Teodor (ed.), *Peasants and Peasant Societies* (Harmondsworth, Penguin Books, 1971).

Shiloh, Ailon (ed.), *Peoples and Cultures of the Middle East* (New York, Random House, 1969).

Smilianskaya, I. M., 'The disintegration of feudal relations in Syria and Lebanon in the middle of the nineteenth century', in Issawi, 1966, pp. 227-47.

Smith, Anthony D., 'Theories and types of nationalism', *Archives européennes de sociologie*, vol. 10 (1969), pp. 119-32.

Smith, Anthony D., *Theories of Nationalism* (London, Duckworth, 1971).

Smith, Anthony D., 'Nationalism and religion: the role of religious reform in the genesis of Arab and Jewish nationalism', *Archives de sciences sociales des religions*, vol. 35 (1973), pp. 23-43.

Smith, Pamela Ann, 'Aspects of class structure in Palestinian society, 1948-1967', in Davis *et al.*, 1975, pp. 98-118.

Sofri, Gianni, *Il modo di produzione asiatico* (Turin, 1969).

Stephens, Robert, *Nasser: a political biography* (Harmondsworth, Penguin Books, 1971).

Stone, Lawrence, 'Theories of revolution', *World Politics*, vol. 18 (1965), pp. 159-76.

Sussnitzki, A. J., 'Ethnic division of labour', in Issawi, 1966, pp. 115-25.

Tambiah, S. J., *World Conqueror and World Renouncer: a study of Buddhism and polity in Thailand against an historical background* (London, Cambridge University Press, 1976).

Taylor, John, 'Review of *Pre-Capitalist Modes of Production*', *Critique of Anthropology*, vol. 1 (1975), pp. 127-55, and vol. 2 (1976), pp. 56-69.

Thornton, T. P. (ed.), *The Third World in Soviet Perspective* (Princeton, NJ, Princeton University Press, 1964).

Tibawi, A. L., 'The American missionaries in Beirut and Butrus Al-Bustānī', *St. Antony's Papers*, no. 16 (1963), pp. 137-82.

Tourneau, Roger Le, Flory, Maurice and Duchac, René, 'Revolution in the Maghreb', in Vatikiotis, 1972, pp. 73-119.

Trotsky, L. D., *History of the Russian Revolution* (London, Gollancz, 1932-3), 3 vols.

Tugendhat, C., *The Multinationals* (Harmondsworth, Penguin Books, 1973).

Turner, Bryan S., 'Sociological founders and precursors: the theories of religion of Emile Durkheim, Fustel de Coulanges and Ibn Khaldun', *Religion: a journal of religion and religions*, vol. 1 (1971), pp. 32-48.

Turner, Bryan S., *Weber and Islam: a critical study* (London, Routledge & Kegan Paul, 1974a).

Turner, Bryan S., 'Islam, capitalism and the Weber theses', *British Journal of Sociology*, vol. 25 (1974b), pp. 230-43.

Turner, Bryan S., 'The concept of social "stationariness": utilitarianism and Marxism', *Science and Society*, vol. 38 (1974c), pp. 3-18.

Turner, Bryan S., 'Avineri's view of Marx's theory of colonialism: Israel', *Science and Society*, vol. 40 (1976), pp. 385-409.

Turner, Bryan S., 'The structuralist critique of Weber's sociology', *British Journal of Sociology*, vol. 28 (1977), pp. 1-16.

Turner, Bryan S. and Hill, M., 'Methodism and the pietist definition of politics: historical development and contemporary evidence', in Hill, 1975, Vol. 8, pp. 159-80.

Ülken, H. Z., 'La sociologie rurale en Turquie', *Sosyoloji Dergisi*, vol. 6 (1950), pp. 104-16.

Urry, John, 'Capital and the state' (British Sociological Association Conference, Sheffield, 1977, mimeo).

van Nieuwenhuijze, C. A. O., *Social Stratification and the Middle East* (Leiden, Brill, 1965).

van Nieuwenhuijze, C. A. O., *Sociology of the Middle East* (Leiden, Brill, 1971).

Vatikiotis, P. J., *Conflicts in the Middle East* (London, Allen & Unwin, 1971).

Vatikiotis, P. J. (ed.), *Revolution in the Middle East and other case studies* (London, Allen & Unwin, 1972).

Venturi, Franco, 'Oriental despotism', *Journal for the History of Ideas*, vol. 24 (1963), pp. 133-42.

Vickery, Susan, 'An analysis of the military in underdeveloped countries: a case study of the ruling-class sociology', in Pateman, 1972, pp. 140-58.

von Grunebaum, G. E., *Classical Islam: a history 600-1258* (London, Allen & Unwin, 1970).

Waines, David, 'Cultural anthropology and Islam: the contribution of G. E. von Grunebaum', *Review of Middle East Studies*, vol. 2 (1976), pp. 113-23.

Wallerstein, Immanuel, *The Modern World-System* (New York, Academic Press, 1974).

Warren, Bill, 'Imperialism and capitalist industrialization', *New Left Review*, no. 81 (1973), pp. 3-44.

Weber, Max, *Economy and Society* (New York, Bedminster Press, 1968), 3 vols.

Weinstock, Nathan, *Le mouvement révolutionnaire arabe* (Paris, Maspero, 1970).

Wertheim, W. F., 'Religion, bureaucracy and economic growth', *Transactions of the Fifth World Congress of Sociology*, vol. 3 (1962), pp. 73-86.

Wertheim, W. F., *Evolution and Revolution* (Harmondsworth, Penguin Books, 1974).

Williams, Raymond, 'Base and superstructure in Marxist cultural theory', *New Left Review*, no. 82 (1973), pp. 3-16.

Wolf, Eric R., *Peasants* (Englewood Cliffs, New Jersey, Prentice Hall, 1966).

Wolf, Eric R., 'On peasant rebellions', in Shanin, 1971, pp. 264-74 (1971a).

Wolf, Eric R., *Peasant Wars of the Twentieth Century* (London, Faber and Faber, 1971b).

Wolin, Sheldon S., *Politics and Vision* (London, Allen & Unwin, 1961).

Woolman, David S., *Rebels in the Rif: Abd El Krim and the Rif Rebellion* (London, Oxford University Press, 1969).

Worsley, Peter, *The Third World* (London, Weidenfeld & Nicolson, 1964).

Zartman, I. William, 'Political science', in Binder, 1976, pp. 265-325.

Zghal, Abdelkader and Karoui, Hachmi, 'Decolonization and social science research: the case of Tunisia', *Middle East Studies Association Bulletin*, vol. 7 (1973), pp. 11-25.

Zubaida, Sami, 'Theories of nationalism' (British Sociological Association, Annual Conference, Sheffield, 1977, mimeo).

Zureik, Elia T., 'From peasantry to proletariat', *Journal of Palestine Studies,* vol. 6 (1976), pp. 39-66.

Index

98 *Marx and the End of Orientalism*

Nasser, G. 21, 47, 54
National Question 60, 66
nationalism 13-14, 53-9, 61-2, 64-5, 82, 84; Arab 28, 53, 60, 66; Jewish 28, 59, 62; Palestinian 62
nations, small 3, 5, 26
nomads 22, 30
nomadism 1, 50-2

objectification 25
oil 23; companies 25
Orientalism 6-9, 14, 31, 53, 59-60, 73, 77, 79-80, 82, 85; Marxist 7; Weber's 7, 9, 45
Orientalist (viewpoint) 39, 41, 43-4, 46, 48, 55, 58, 65, 67, 70, 78-81

Palestine 4, 28, 59, 79
patrimonialism 1, 45, 82
peasants/peasantry 4, 19, 22, 28, 30, 45, 50, 55, 64, 72, 74
Portugal 78
Poulantzas, N. 35-6, 64, 72, 76-8, 83-4
prebendalism 45, 50-2, 83
production: forces of 33-4, 49, 74, 82; means of 16, 26; petty commodity 23, 31, 51; relations of 16-17, 26-7, 32-4, 44, 61, 74, 82
profit 15

rational law 11
rebellion 68, 79
reification 25
Renan, E. 56
rent 3, 33, 37, 45, 50
revolution 66-70, 72-3, 81-2; Algerian 70, 73; Arab 68; bourgeois 65, 67, 72, 74, 82; Egyptian 69; French 68, 72; no revolutions thesis 67-8, 70, 72-3, 76-8; Saudi 73; social 7, 67; sociology of 73, 76
rights 3, 22, 33, 69-72, 75, 77-8, 81
Rodinson, M. 2, 7
Russia 1, 68

Sadat, A. 21
Saudi Arabia 51
secularisation 53, 57-8, 65-6, 82
sedentarisation 23, 30-1, 51
serfdom 17, 74
Sharia (Seray) 6, 40
sipahis 50
slavery 17, 52, 64, 74, 77
Smith, A. 58, 60

social formation: concrete 35; and conjunctures 85; and modes of production 50, 75-6, 84; and society 35
socialism 4, 8, 59, 70, 76; Arab 79; Israeli 4, 25; Jewish 4
society: Arab 24, 27, 74; Asiatic 45, 82; civil 42, 71; backward 10-11, 79; underdeveloped 12, 18, 23, 47, 52
sociology 83; bourgeois 14, 77, 82; Durkheimian 2; Weberian 83-5
Spain 73, 78
Spencer, H. 67
Stalin, J. 42
state 30, 33-4, 45, 47, 51, 68, 72, 74-5, 78, 84; absolutist 36; Christian 3; interventionist 14, 16; nightwatchman 14; Oriental 27; post-colonial 21, 24, 64, 75-6
stratification 4, 41, 43, 46, 49
structures (economic, ideological and political) 33, 42, 65, 66, 76
superstructure 44, 59, 62-4, 80, 84
surplus value 15
Syria 13, 20, 28, 69

tax/rent couple 33-4, 37, 45
technological determinism 33, 49
timar 50
Tunisia 2, 41
Turkey 1, 2, 13, 30, 41
Turner, B. S. 9

ulama 6, 40, 43
underdevelopment 10, 14, 17, 19, 32
United States 12
utilitarians 15, 71

vatan 55
Vatikiotis, P. J. 58, 60, 68, 72-3
villages (self-sufficient) 14, 42, 54
von Grunebaum, G. E. 6

wafq 6, 22, 46
Waines, D. 6
Wallerstein, I. 83
war: First World 60; Second World 18, 23; Six Days 25, 29, 31; Yom Kippur 25, 79
Weber, M. 44, 46, 62, 83-4
West Bank 28-9, 30-2
Worsley, P. 57

Zartman, I. W. 67-8
Zionism 3-4, 25, 28, 54, 58-9
Zubaida, S. 61-2, 84